Supporting Disabled Students in Higher Education

Supporting Disabled Students in Higher Education is a practical and inclusive handbook designed to ensure disabled students are supported in their journey through mainstream higher education. Informed by case studies, this essential guide highlights how this can be achieved through the adoption of practical, reasonable adjustments. Coupled with recommendations for best practice across higher education, this book outlines experiences and barriers to inclusion and provides detailed guidance for inclusive practices including adjustments to accommodation, accessing physical and virtual learning spaces, teaching activities, developing the curriculum and assessment.

Written by an experienced dyslexia and disability coordinator within higher education, chapters encourage readers to develop a greater understanding of the impact that disabilities may have on students' academic progress. Areas explored include:

- Specific learning difficulties (SpLD)
- Mental health conditions
- Visually impaired and blind students
- Deaf and hearing-impaired students
- Physical impairments
- Long-term medical conditions

This book lays out the step-by-step process to enable effective communication between disability staff, academic staff and students and is a crucial guide for anyone with an interest in promoting and facilitating accessibility, inclusion and widening participation in higher education.

Stephen Campbell is the Manager of Disability Services at Leeds Trinity University, UK.

Supporting Disabled Students in Higher Education

The Reasonable Adjustments Handbook

Stephen Campbell

Routledge
Taylor & Francis Group
LONDON AND NEW YORK

Designed cover image: © Olga Siletskaya / Getty Images

First published 2023
by Routledge
4 Park Square, Milton Park, Abingdon, Oxon OX14 4RN

and by Routledge
605 Third Avenue, New York, NY 10158

Routledge is an imprint of the Taylor & Francis Group, an informa business

© 2023 Stephen Campbell

The right of Stephen Campbell to be identified as author of this work has been asserted in accordance with sections 77 and 78 of the Copyright, Designs and Patents Act 1988.

All rights reserved. No part of this book may be reprinted or reproduced or utilised in any form or by any electronic, mechanical, or other means, now known or hereafter invented, including photocopying and recording, or in any information storage or retrieval system, without permission in writing from the publishers.

Trademark notice: Product or corporate names may be trademarks or registered trademarks, and are used only for identification and explanation without intent to infringe.

British Library Cataloguing-in-Publication Data
A catalogue record for this book is available from the British Library

Names: Campbell, Stephen, author.
Title: Supporting disabled students in higher education: the reasonable adjustments handbook / Stephen Campbell.
Description: Abingdon, Oxon; New York, NY: Routledge, 2023. | Includes bibliographical references and index.
Identifiers: LCCN 2022057500 (print) | LCCN 2022057501 (ebook) | ISBN 9781032109701 (hardback) | ISBN 9781032122922 (paperback) | ISBN 9781003223962 (ebook)
Subjects: LCSH: College students with disabilities—Services for. | Learning disabled—Education (Higher) | Inclusive education.
Classification: LCC LC4818.38 .C36 2023 (print) | LCC LC4818.38 (ebook) | DDC 371.9/0474—dc23/eng/20230301
LC record available at https://lccn.loc.gov/2022057500
LC ebook record available at https://lccn.loc.gov/2022057501

ISBN: 978-1-032-10970-1 (hbk)
ISBN: 978-1-032-12292-2 (pbk)
ISBN: 978-1-003-22396-2 (ebk)

DOI: 10.4324/9781003223962

Typeset in Galliard
by codeMantra

Contents

	Introduction	1
1	Specific learning difficulties (SpLD)	12
2	Mental health	38
3	Visually impaired/blind students	61
4	D/deaf hearing impaired	80
5	Physical impairments	94
6	Students with long-term medical conditions	108
7	Disability, illness and taboo	120
	Conclusion	129
	Index	133

Introduction

What is disability?

If you were asked 'What is disability?', how would you answer? This is not the same as being asked 'what are disabilities?', as you might respond quite reasonably that disabilities can include blindness, hearing impairment, physical impairment, dyslexia, depression or epilepsy to name a few. But to be asked 'what is disability?' is to be asked to reflect on what you think you know about disability and why. Given the prominence of disabled and impaired characters who have regularly featured in popular culture, we can assume that most people will hold some notions about disabled people. But whether those notions have been informed by more than the fictional or dramatic representations of Shakespeare's villainous Richard the Third, Dickens' pitiable Tiny Tim, George RR Martin's scheming Tyrion Lannister or just about every James Bond villain will depend upon other factors that may have informed one's understanding of disability. Certainly, personal, direct experience with disabled people, professional training and basic research can help form a wider awareness of disability beyond cultural references and prevalent social attitudes. It would be unusual, therefore, to come across an individual with no opinions about disability, so we can presume at least that a significant proportion of the population could attempt to answer the question 'what is disability?'

Although this book's overall purpose is to recommend practical advice on higher education (HE) disability inclusion, it would be wrong to think that material adjustments alone constitute the substance of disability support. If this were the case, then disability could easily be understood as simply an individual limitation, something remediated through the practical intervention of a non-disabled professional. To take such a position would immediately identify any potential problem within the body of the disabled individual. What is disability? Well, surely it must be something intrinsic to the disabled person themselves? Something biological perhaps? This book does not intend merely to provide a list of possible adjustments for disabled students; it also seeks to challenge the belief that disabled individuals are the cause of non-disabled people's problems,

DOI: 10.4324/9781003223962-1

and that we all share the responsibility of ensuring greater access and inclusion for disabled students. In other words, to change how we act towards disabled people means changing the way many of us think about disabled people. Which of course raises the question, what do we think about disabled people?

The answer, according to the Scope's 2018 Disability Perception Gap Policy Report (Dixon et al., 2018), isn't good. In the UK, one in five non-disabled people believe there is a lot of prejudice against disabled persons. This contrasts with one in three disabled people who are strongly of the opinion that negative attitudes and prejudice remain a major problem for them. The report goes on to state that this 'could be because non-disabled people are simply unaware of the levels of prejudice faced by disabled people, and potentially aren't conscious of their own prejudicial attitudes towards disabled people'. Prejudicial attitudes can include audible sighs and tuts when asked to make even a modest adjustment for a disabled person, allowing doors to swing closed in the face of a disabled individual, ignoring the disabled person altogether or talking over them to address a partner or carer. Or simply to hold low academic expectations of disabled students. Such prejudices inevitably influence the whole life experience of the disabled community in all areas, including work, employment, housing, health care and indeed education. What disability is, therefore, is fundamentally a civil rights issue.

Disability and civil rights

Today, it is estimated that disabled people constitute about 15% of the world's population, which means that disabled people are part of a significant albeit minority global demographic (International Labour Organization, 2020). According to the United Nations, people with disabilities are the world's largest minority group (World Health Organisation, 2021). The United Nations (2021a) has estimated that 20% of the world's poorest people are disabled in some form, and that their physical or learning impairments are exacerbated by social taboos and attitudes surrounding chronic illness and disability. Across all nations, disabled people face daily challenges for inclusion in education, employment, leisure and housing, and any autonomy for disabled people to choose how to access vital education, social and health services is often undermined by institutional barriers and political legislation privileging the voices of medical professionals or legislators over that of disabled people themselves. UNESCO (2021), for example, highlights that 90% of disabled children and young people in developing countries do not attend school, while the International Labour Organization (2020) found that unemployment among disabled people stands at 80% in some countries.

In 2006, the United Nations drafted the Convention on the Rights of Persons with Disabilities (CRPD) as an international human rights treaty intended to protect the rights and dignity of people with disabilities. By 2020, the treaty had 163 signatories and was in fact the first human rights treaty of the twenty-first century. The purpose of the Convention is to 'promote, protect and ensure the full and equal enjoyment of all human rights and fundamental freedoms by all persons with disabilities, and to promote respect for their inherent dignity'. The Convention was the result of many decades of campaigning from disability groups protesting against what they saw as oppressive and unequal treatment by governments, health services, educational and medical institutions in systematically depriving them of personal agency, freedom of choice and dignity.

In the UK, there are 14.6 million disabled people (Scope, 2021). In terms of employment, disabled people are 14% more likely to work part-time than non-disabled people and even more likely to retire early. Even taking account of the impact a disability or health condition may have upon a disabled person's ability to work, nonetheless attitudinal and social factors serve to perpetuate the disadvantages experienced by disabled workers. In many instances, disabled people have been discouraged from entering particular professions resulting in an over-representation in low-income employment. And even for disabled graduates, it is not uncommon to experience similar glass ceilings, with a considerable number of workers overlooked or discouraged from applying for more senior positions. Disabled workers are 50% 'more likely to have suffered unfairness, discrimination, bullying or harassment at work compared with non-disabled people' (Shakespeare, 2018: 23). As well as finding that a vast majority of non-disabled people greatly underestimated the number of disabled people in the UK, amongst employers and the workforce, disabled people are less likely to be viewed as equally productive than their non-disabled counterparts, irrespective of what formal training or high level of qualification they may have achieved.

This poses particular challenges for universities. Increasingly in the UK, especially in England and Wales, higher education institutions are required to make public annual statistics detailing their respective graduate outcomes, one of which includes entry into professional employment. If a university's position on the national league tables depends on the number of students graduating into professional careers, then the necessity to ensure the inclusion and academic success of the increasing number of disabled students is paramount. Yet, as with employment, so with higher education. Although disabled students' participation in HE has increased from 8.1% to 13.2% between 2010 and 2017 (Office for Students, 2019), research suggests that 40 months after leaving higher education, the number of disabled graduates in a professional or managerial role was significantly less than their non-disabled peers. *The Institute for Employment Studies Review of Support for Disabled Students in Higher Education in England* also revealed not only that disabled students are more likely to drop out of university than non-disabled students, but for those that do complete their course, they are more likely to graduate with lower grades. This was reiterated in the recent House of Commons report *Support for disabled students in higher education in England*, which stated bleakly that:

> …disabled students in higher education have somewhat worse outcomes from higher education than non-disabled students. Students with a

disability are more likely to drop-out of courses and those that finish their degree tend to have lower degree results.

(Hubble and Bolton, 2021)

The predicament facing higher education providers is how to reconcile the support and inclusion needs of disabled students with the growing requirement for universities to act as preparatory organisations for entry into employment. Focusing upon diagnosed impairments and responding to individual needs is certainly a way to ensure bespoke support is put in place for disabled students. But this approach can run the risk of reinforcing a certain dependency on those whose responsibility it is to coordinate disability inclusion rather than to look more holistically at institutional practices. It is in this human rights context, and in the spirit of egalitarianism, that higher education institutions must endeavour to create learning environments that are accessible, supportive and inclusive for disabled students. What this requires is a shift away from thinking about disability as a deficit students bring with them into university, to an understanding that disability must be addressed institutionally.

Disability as social issue – the medical and social models

Disability is not just a medical diagnosis. Anyone new to the academic field of disability studies, or to the health, education and social care professions, may assume that to be 'disabled' is to lack capacity of some kind. Disability in this sense comes from within the disabled person, it is intrinsic to them and is the primary cause of their disablement. In this respect, disability is a condition that once identified can be treated, often by medical or health professionals, certainly by specialists with expertise in the area, from which the disabled individual adopts the role of passive receiver of specialist treatment. Being disabled from this perspective is largely to be at the mercy of professions, systems and policies that effectively remove personal agency away from the disabled individual and into the hands of others. These others have variously included over the years doctors, law makers, physiotherapists, specialist educators and other specially trained diagnosticians, educators and professionals. This framing of disability as a predominantly health or medical issue has come to be known today as the medical model of disability. This is a model by which disability is directly the result of a physical condition, inherent to the person and which causes a reduction in their quality of life. A person who uses a wheelchair, for example, is disabled according to the medical model because of the physical impairment preventing them from leading an otherwise active and engaged life. The medical model, however, is much deeper than this. In addition to the physical limitations placed on them by their conditions, further disablement is caused by socially prevalent attitudes that serve to reinforce stereotypical and prejudicial beliefs about disabled people. If it is widely accepted that a disabled person cannot do something such as drive a car, ride a bike, access buildings, etc., then it logically (and erroneously) follows that any exclusion from certain aspects of life is because of the condition alone. Putting it simply, while disabled people have access to specialists for everyday assistance, there is no reason to believe the rest of society has any obligation to help. From this framing of disability comes exclusion from employment, education, housing, health care and many other aspects of daily living most of us take for granted. For those disabled individuals who came to see their treatments and care plans and social exclusions as a system designed specifically to force them to the margins of society arose the idea that the medical model was not there to assist but rather to oppress. What was required, therefore, was a new way of thinking about disability, one not informed by medical orthodoxy, but instead from the civil rights movement of the middle twentieth century.

Disability emerged as a major issue in both developing and developed countries, thanks to effective disability campaigners and organisations. Created in 1972 The Union of the Physically Impaired Against Segregation (UPIAS) was one of the first disability rights organisations in the United Kingdom. UPIAS set out the principles that in time led to the development of what we now call 'the social model of disability', a principle that intended to draw a distinction between impairment and disability. A reconceptualised (social model of) disability argues that rather than disability being caused by the condition or impairment, to be disabled is to be excluded, marginalised and disadvantaged from society because of prejudicial attitudes and practices that work against the interests of disabled people. The UPIAS policy statement read:

> What we are interested in, are ways of changing our conditions of life, and thus overcoming the disabilities which are imposed on top of our physical impairments by the way this society is organised to exclude us.

Similarly, the British Council of Organisations of Disabled People (BCODP), founded in 1981, also believed that what disabled people needed was an organised mass movement to campaign for legal and social change. Disability, in the words of sociologist and disability campaigner Tom Shakespeare, is 'both extremely interesting and rather complicated' (Shakespeare, 2018: 1). To disability rights campaigner and academic Michael Oliver, disability is very much external to the individual and located within 'the physical and social environments' (Oliver, 1990: 7). In other words, how we understand disability rather depends on how we understand society and the hidden mechanisms that serve to exclude or marginalise disabled people. For disability sociologists, one of those hidden social mechanisms is a society's values and deeply held beliefs about disabled people.

In attempting to understand disability sociologically rather than medically, we must consider the twin notions of disablement and disablism, or ableism. *Disablement* is the state of being disabled or the experiences that arise from becoming disabled. Understanding that disability is the complex interplay of impairment, inaccessible environments and social attitudes regarding disabled people, then we can see that disability is a 'cultural concept' (Goodley, 2016), one that once recognised can be challenged. The challenge itself comes from recognising that disablement derives from **disablism**, which according to Abberley (1987) is the cultural, social and economic conditions of which disablement is a consequence. This is an important distinction to make as social attitudes continue to play a significant role in the disablement of disabled individuals. Disablism, therefore, is a term that can be used to describe prejudice, discrimination and oppression against disabled people, of which its resistance by organisations such as UPIAS and BCODP has greatly influenced the way disability policies and inclusive practices continue to shape the lives of disabled people. The social model, however, is not without its critics; it has been challenged on the grounds that the realities of personal pain, fatigue, depression and internalised oppression are neglected within it, and that it deterministically fails to acknowledge the ability of disabled people to challenge institutional constraints (Borsay, 2004). The challenge, then, comes from being able to recognise the intersection between personal experience and the necessity of delivering social change 'by addressing the concrete reality of discrimination' (Borsay, 2004: 13).

If Goodley and Abberley are correct in their assertions that disability is a social concept, then like all social concepts, it has not come to exist in a vacuum. It has emerged and developed throughout history. How we think about, respond to and represent disability are embedded in our collective cultural consciousness through a combination of representation and misrepresentation. Indeed, the growing emergence of disability studies as a multi-disciplinary field has seen disability emerge more prominently in areas of enquiry such as history, cultural studies, medical humanities, sociology and art. Historian Phillipa Vincent-Connolly's research, for example, has highlighted the lives of disabled people in Tudor England, while writers such as Elsa Sjunneson and Pippa Stacey (2020) have reflected on their own experiences of being Deafblind and chronically ill, respectively. Similarly, academics such as Temple Grandin (Grandin and Panek, 2013) and Sandra Beale-Ellis (2017) have combined their personal experiences of being autistic with grounded research to produce works that are as autobiographical as they are academic. The driver for greater representation across academia and wider society is nicely summarised by Elsa Sjunneson: '… our culture relentlessly seeks two things: simplicity of understanding and the ability to sort into groups. Disability is a broad category, containing millions of individuals, and yet we treat it as a monolith, even today' (2021: 9). The history of disability, then, is complex and varied, but certainly one with a common theme, namely that 'Nondisabled people frequently appoint themselves the disability police' (Sjunneson, 2021: 6).

Disability – a brief history of prejudice

The idea that disabled people are subject to the whims of nondisabled people is not new in history. Within the Judeo-Christian traditions, the Bible variously suggests that certain impairments are a punishment from God, with the book of Leviticus especially passing judgement on a range of impairments and defects:
The Lord said to Moses,

> Say to Aaron: 'For the generations to come none of your descendants who has a blemish may come near to offer the food of his God. No man who has any blemish may come near: no man who is blind or lame, disfigured or deformed; no man with a crippled foot or hand, or who is a hunchback or a dwarf, or who has any eye defect, or who has festering or running sores or damaged testicles'.
> (Lev. 20:16–20, NIV)

The understanding of 'blemish' here is synonymous with unclean, the legacy of which, according to Belser (2019: 355), is that 'conventional readings of these texts have left in place power dynamics that presume the inferiority of the disabled body'. The notion that disabled bodies within biblical and pre-monotheistic cultures are bound to those society's purity laws (Hentrich, 2004) is the central issue relating to disabled people's social acceptance throughout most of history. And yet, the problem with social acceptance is that the rules governing who is and is not acceptable are rather vague or bound up within centuries of social anxieties. Lindsey Fitzharris points out that facially wounded soldiers during the First World War were often shunned by their communities not just because of the feelings of revulsion evoked by their injuries but also because of long-standing historical prejudices against such disabilities. 'For centuries', she points out, 'a marked face was interpreted as an outward sign of moral or intellectual degeneracy. People often associated facial irregularities with the devastating effects of disease, such as leprosy and syphilis, or with corporal punishment, wickedness and sin' (Fitzharris, 2022: 12). Kate Lister similarly draws our attention to the arbitrariness of social exclusion in many societies particularly as it relates to sex and bodily autonomy. The practice of banishing menstruating women from the family home because of the belief that menstruating blood and therefore menstruating women are impure is, according to Lister, 'to prevent others from being polluted' (Lister, 2020: 291). Such (extreme) practices illustrate that historical and cultural attitudes towards bodily non-conformity are often met with often quite severe punitive legislative sanctions, with the sanctions themselves often favouring banishment of one kind or another. In 1881, for example, Chicago's City Council passed a law barring all "diseased, maimed, mutilated" people from the city's public streets in what became known as one in a series of 'ugly laws' across the United States.

In this sense, we again come back to disability and health as somehow conflated with personal morality and the idea that being disabled or unhealthy 'carries with it an element of personal failure' (Morrall, 2009: 43).

Such perceived threats to social integrity have historically framed much of the life experiences of disabled people. The 1601 Poor Law Act and explosion of workhouses across Britain from the eighteenth century acted as highly effective drivers of incarceration for those classified as elderly, sick or 'infirm'. Similarly, the 1845 Lunacy Act confined to asylums anyone who was classified as an 'idiot', a 'lunatic' or considered not to be of sound mind. Despite the perceived differences between the three categories, all were brought under the wider term of 'insane' and thus removed from society into the asylum system. Institutionalisation was not necessarily reserved for those we now recognise as having mental health conditions; there was very little to distinguish mental and physical disabilities at the time, meaning that individuals with sight loss, cerebral palsy and learning difficulties were likewise deprived of their freedoms.

The cultural influences of institutions, whether medical or in time educational, have in many ways reinforced disparaging and negative ideas of disability. Today, terms such as 'idiot' or 'lunatic' or even worse are not used unless to insult, and the fact they derive from formerly official classifications of disorders tells us much about the way society continues to view disability. The history of disability, then, is a history of marginalisation. The voices of disabled individuals throughout history are mostly heard, if they are heard at all, through the prism of official records, medical documents or the diaries of others.

By the time the UK introduced the Disability Discrimination Act (1995) followed by the Equality Act (2010), disability-as-civil-rights had been accepted enough for the principles of the social model to inform the new legislation. Under the Equality Act (2010) certainly, 'disability' was classified not to incarcerate individuals but instead to protect their rights as citizens. Disability is one of nine 'protected characteristics' in which it is now illegal to discriminate against, with the additional legislative requirement for institutions to include disabled people through means of 'reasonable adjustments'.

UK legislation and statutory requirements

The primary piece of legislation in the UK relating to disability inclusion is the Equality Act 2010. The Equality Act 2010 updates and consolidates the various Acts that previously formed the basis of the country's anti-discrimination laws. As well as the Disability Discrimination Act 1995, the Equality Act also consolidated into it the Equal Pay Act 1970, the Sex Discrimination Act 1975, and the Race Relations Act 1976. There are nine protected characteristics under the Equality Act, meaning that it is illegal to discriminate anyone because of:

- Age
- Gender reassignment

- Being married or in a civil partnership
- Being pregnant or on maternity leave
- Disability
- Race including colour, nationality, ethnic or national origin
- Religion or belief
- Sex
- Sexual orientation

'Disability' under the Equality Act is defined in the following way:

> You're disabled under the Equality Act 2010 if you have a physical or mental impairment that has a 'substantial' and 'long-term' negative effect on your ability to do normal daily activities.

- 'Substantial' is more than minor or trivial, e.g. it takes much longer than it usually would to complete a daily task like getting dressed
- 'Long-term' means 12 months or more, e.g. a breathing condition that develops as a result of a lung infection

Reasonable adjustments

Organisations such as schools, colleges, universities, as well as employers, local authorities and shops are legally required to remove any barriers to inclusion that may exist as a direct or indirect result of a person's disability. The Equality Act 2010 calls this the duty to make reasonable adjustments, the purpose of which is to ensure disabled people are provided with equal services and opportunities as non-disabled people.

The question as to what exactly is reasonable or unreasonable is not something that can be easily answered. To put in place reasonable adjustments for university students, consider the following. Firstly, The Equality Act says that a disabled individual should never be asked to pay for their own adjustments. This necessarily means universities and higher education providers must allocate an annual budget specifically for disability support. Of course, this is relative to the financial circumstances of each university, which secondly means that universities must take account of their size, the resources that are available (financial or otherwise) and the overall cost of the adjustment.

Consider also whether the adjustment is practical. This is not the same as deciding if it is inconvenient. As with the financial implications of the adjustment, it must be considered whether something too logistically impractical crosses over into the unreasonable category. Remember, however, that you are not looking for reasons not to make adjustments. The purpose of reasonable adjustments is to identify potential instances of discrimination and exclusion against disabled people and to take the necessary measures to ensure that the teaching and learning environment is accessible.

What follows are suggested recommendations for reasonable adjustments in higher education. The book is intended to guide HE staff, and students, through the process of putting in place adjustments without being excessively exhaustive or prescriptive. Each chapter focuses upon a particular disability/impairment which some readers may find useful. I am mindful there may be some disagreement of how some disabilities have been classified (ADHD as a learning difficulty, for example, has elsewhere been classified as a behavioural disorder or a mental health condition; mental health include four conditions against an array of other possible diagnoses), or that some individual problems faced by staff responding to disabled students' needs are not specifically included. To that I would say that this book is not intended to be used as a care plan or to provide advice that is not related to higher education student inclusion. Instead, I hope the book will provide some useful suggestions for reasonable adjustments and tips for thinking about disability as something that, according to the social model, stems from an unadjusted and inaccessible environment.

References

Abberley, P. (1987). Performing the body, creating culture. In K. Davis (ed), *Embodied practices: Feminist perspectives on the body.* (pp. 41–58). Sage.

Beale-Ellis, S. (2017). *Sensing the city: An autistic perspective.* Jessica Kingsley Publishers.

Belser, J.W. (2019). Priestly aesthetics: Disability and bodily difference in Leviticus 21. *Interpretation*, 73(4), pp. 355–366.

Borsay, A. (2004). *Disability and social policy in Britain since 1750: A history of exclusion.* Bloomsbury Publishing.

Dixon, S., Smith, C. and Touchet, A. (2018). The disability perception gap. Policy Report.

Equality Act (2010). Definition of disability under the Equality Act 2010. https://www.gov.uk/definition-of-disability-under-equality-act-2010#:~:text=You're%20disabled%20under%20the, to%20do%20normal%20daily%20activities.

Fitzharris, L. (2022). *The Facemaker.* Allen Lane.

Goodley, D. (2016). *Disability studies: An interdisciplinary introduction.* Sage.

Grandin, T. and Panek, R. (2013). *The autistic brain: Thinking across the spectrum.* Houghton Mifflin Harcourt.

Hentrich, T. (2004). The purity laws as a source for conflict in the Old and New Testament. *Annual of the Japanese Biblical Institute*, 30, pp. 5–21.

Hubble and Bolton. (2021). Support for disabled students in higher education in England. House of Commons Library. Number 8716, 22 February 2021.

International Labour Organization. (2020). International day of persons with disabilities: How disabilities affect labor market outcomes. https://ilostat.ilo.org/international-day-of-persons-with-disabilities-how-disability-affects-labour-market-outcomes/

Lister, K. (2020). *A curious history of sex.* Unbound Publishing.

Morrall, P. (2009). *Sociology and health: An introduction.* Routledge.

Office for Students. (2019). Disabled Students. https://www.officeforstudents.org.uk/advice-and-guidance/promoting-equal-opportunities/effective-practice/disabled-students/

Oliver, M. (1990). *The politics of disablement.* Macmillan.

'Disability Facts and Figures'. (2021). https://www.scope.org.uk/media/disability-facts-figures/

Shakespeare, T. (2018). *Disability: The basics.* Routledge.

Sjunneson, E. (2021). *Being seen: One deafblind woman's fight to end ableism.* Tiller Press.

Stacey, P. (2020). University and chronic illness: A survival guide. Daisa & Co.

UNESCO (2021). Access for Persons with Disabilities. https://en.unesco.org/themes/access-persons-disabilities#:~:text=Access%20for%20Persons%20with%20Disabilities,Access%20for%20persons&text=As%20the%20United%20Nations%20agency,with%20Disabilities%2C%20adopted%20in%202006.

Union of the Physically Impaired against Segregation UPIAS and the Disability Alliance. (1976). Fundamental Principles of Disability. In National Disability Arts Collection and Archive (2021). https://the-ndaca.org/resources/audio-described-gallery/fundamental-principles-of-disability/

United Nations (2021a). Department of Economic and Social Affairs, Disability. https://www.un.org/development/desa/disabilities/resources/factsheet-on-persons-with-disabilities.html

United Nations (2021b). International Day od Person's with Disabilities. https://www.un.org/en/observances/day-of-persons-with-disabilities/background#:~:text=Persons%20with%20disabilities%2C%20%E2%80%9Cthe%20world's,poverty%20than%20people%20without%20disabilities.

Vincent-Connolly, P. (2021). *Disability and the tudors: All the king's fools.* Pen & Sword.

World Health Organisation. (2021). Factsheet on Persons with Disabilities | United Nations Enable. https://www.un.org/development/desa/disabilities/resources/-factsheet-on-persons-with-disabilities.html

Chapter 1
Specific learning difficulties (SpLD)

Case study – Barry

Barry enrolled at university to study business and economics. He had never previously been tested for dyslexia nor received any additional support while at school and college. During his first year, Barry noticed that he was struggling academically; he was having difficulty following some lectures, meeting deadlines and remembering much of what he had read from his core reading list. For some reason, his grades were significantly below what he expected; it was as if he couldn't convey enough of what he did know to achieve better marks. These initial experiences left him feeling demotivated and stressed, which in time also had an adverse effect on his academic performance. By the end of his first year, Barry was giving serious consideration to dropping out. It was Barry's personal tutor who suggested he might want to consider speaking with the university's disability services. It may be, he explained, that Barry was dyslexic. This came a surprise to Barry, who had never thought of himself as needing support before. But he decided to give it a go. The disability service staff arranged for an initial screening, the results of which indicated a likelihood of dyslexia. From there, Barry arranged with the assistance of the disability services team to undergo a full educational psychological assessment. The report came back confirming dyslexia. From there the university put in a series of reasonable adjustments for Barry. He was allowed extra time in exams, permission to record lectures and teaching sessions as well as extended borrowing periods for library loans. Barry also could access specialist 1:1 study skills to help develop his reading and note taking strategies, essay structure, exam preparation and time management. Eventually, Barry felt more supported by his institution and more in control of his workload.

What is dyslexia?

Dyslexia translates from Greek as 'difficulty with words'. The term was first introduced in 1887 by German ophthalmologist Rudulf Berlin who had observed the difficulties faced by some of his adult patients in reading the printed word. Berlin surmised that, in the absence of any immediate explanation to account for such anomalous literacy deficits, the cause of the problem must lie in the brain. At about the same time, German neurologist Adolf Kussmaul used the term 'word blindness' to describe adults with similar reading problems whom he observed also experiencing difficulties acquiring basic literacy skills. At the time, of course, neither could have known for sure what may have caused this strange reading difficulty. But given that their patients were of average intelligence, had received a level of education and schooling comparable to their peers, yet whose ability to read and comprehend printed material was mysteriously compromised, the notion that this singular condition was inherent became firmly established.

Over a century since Berlin first observed instances of impaired reading acquisition from otherwise averagely intelligent patients, recent neuroimaging techniques have yielded sufficient data to bolster the original suggestion that the problem may indeed lie within the brain. So robust is the evidence for a neurobiological origin of dyslexia that the evidence has prompted some researchers to state confidentially that with neurological data 'educators can know how the brain processes word information with little room for debate' (Kearns et al., 2018: 178).

One could be mistaken for thinking that between Berlin and Kussmaul's initial speculation to the present day that what we know about dyslexia is that it is only a 'difficulty with words'. To an extent, this is broadly still the case, with Shaywitz and Shaywitz (2008: 1333) asserting that dyslexia 'reflects an unexpected difficulty in reading in children and adults who appear to have all the factors present (intelligence, motivation, exposure to reasonable reading instruction) that are necessary to turn print into meaning'.

More recent research has revealed that what it is, is a series of cognitive impairments adversely affecting multiple skills to varying degrees (Fiorello et al., 2006). The British Dyslexia Association describes the condition as 'a learning difference which primarily affects reading and writing skills. However, it does not only affect these skills. Dyslexic people may have difficulty processing and remembering information they see and hear, which can affect learning and the acquisition of literacy skills. Dyslexia can also impact on other areas such as organisational skills' (British Dyslexia Association (BDA), 2021). To reinforce this point, the BDA have adopted the Rose (2009) definition of dyslexia:

> Dyslexia is a learning difficulty that primarily affects the skills involved in accurate and fluent word reading and spelling. Characteristic features of dyslexia are difficulties in phonological awareness, verbal memory and verbal processing speed. Dyslexia occurs across the range of intellectual abilities. It is best thought of as a continuum, not a distinct category, and there are no clear cut-off points. Co-occurring difficulties may be seen in aspects of language, motor co-ordination, mental calculation, concentration and personal organisation, but these are not, by themselves, markers of dyslexia. A good indication of the severity and persistence of dyslexic difficulties can be gained by examining how the individual responds or has responded to well-founded intervention.

What this immediately tells us is that there are primary characteristics associated with dyslexia that can form the basis of a tailored programme of support. But for the right adjustments to be made, it is important to know not just what dyslexia is, but what the potential barriers to learning may be.

Dyslexia – barriers to learning

Primary symptoms of dyslexia are those which form the basis of an educational psychological diagnosis (phonological processing, working memory, etc.), while secondary symptoms include what can be described as the lived experience, for example, self-perception, self-esteem, anxiety and low motivation. While an understanding of what dyslexia is rightly focuses on its status as a neurological difficulty, the importance of understanding that barriers to learning are caused by a combination of factors must not be overlooked.

Primary symptoms of dyslexia

General characteristic

Literacy and language-related skills

Written work can be poorly organised. Ideas may not be articulated coherently, and overall structure may lack fluency. It is likely there will be many spelling mistakes throughout, and vocabulary, especially subject-specific terminology, may be limited. Dyslexic students may have difficulties translating orthographic representations of written sounds (letters/graphemes) into their corresponding sound, e.g. ă pat; oi noise; û urge.

Depending on the severity of dyslexia and quality of previous education/support, there may be many examples of phonetic or inconsistent spelling of unfamiliar words.

Some students with dyslexia may also be susceptible to visual discomfort while reading for long periods of time. Eyestrain and headaches are not uncommon.

Phonological processing – difficulties processing speech sounds. Students with dyslexia-related phonological weaknesses may experience difficulties manipulating the individual units of sounds of word (phonemes). Associated with this are potential difficulties aurally distinguishing similar sounding phonemes, e.g. 'put' 'but', 'pebble' 'bubble'.

Working memory/information processing. Working memory is the ability to hold and manipulate information over short periods of time. For example, listening to, remembering and following instructions; remembering questions long enough to formulate answers; following the gist of conversations particularly during group discussions; applying learning to new situations.

Dyslexic students may need longer than their non-dyslexic peers to take in and make sense of new information. Individual students will differ to varying degrees, but to an extent, there may be delays in when they feel confident enough to respond to any new information that is presented to them. As processing speed is about making sense of information, students may experience problems processing visual, auditory and/or verbal information.

Self-management/personal organisation. Cognitively, dyslexic students have weak executive functioning; this manifests as difficulty being able to manage several tasks at once and prioritising short- to medium-term activities. It may also result in poor time management, difficulty keeping to schedules and working on multiple assignments simultaneously.

Secondary symptoms of dyslexia

It would not be accurate to say that the stresses and anxieties experienced by dyslexic students are the symptoms of an internal condition that exists independent of any social context. As with all learning difficulties, an inextricable relationship exists between the condition and its interaction with the social, emotional and learning environments of the individual, meaning that although general characteristics of dyslexia can be identified, the extent of their affect is not uniformly the same. Personal circumstances, background, quality of education and individual resilience all play a part in exacerbating or mitigating the condition. The secondary symptoms of dyslexia play into much broader issues of personal experiences, particularly how the learning difficulties faced by students may have come up against unhelpful, antagonistic or inhibiting institutional or social barriers. Students with dyslexia feel increased anxiety levels because of their literacy difficulties, rather than any genetic and environmental factors (Willcutt and Pennington, 2000; International Dyslexia Association, 2021). This is a fundamentally important aspect to consider when putting measures in place to support students whose mental health and wellbeing are directly driven by the extent to which they feel comfortable and accommodated on their course.

For many dyslexic people, their abilities will develop over the course of their lives, yet for most, they will invariably experience higher than average levels of anxiety (Carroll and Iles, 2006).

General characteristic

Anxiety. Individuals with dyslexia may experience marked anxiety in situations in which they feel they will make mistakes, be ridiculed or made to feel foolish in front of others. Stress and anxiety increase when we're in situations over which we have little or no control. All people, young and old, can experience overwhelming stress and exhibit signs of anxiety, but children, adolescents and adults with dyslexia are particularly vulnerable (International Dyslexia Association).

Low self-esteem. Many individuals do not fully understand the nature of their learning difficulties, and as a result tend to blame themselves for their own difficulties. Years of self-doubt and self-recrimination may erode a person's self-esteem, making them less able to tolerate the challenges of school, work or social interactions and more therefore become stressed and anxious (International Dyslexia Association).

Catastrophising. Catastrophising is when a person believes in the worst-case scenario of a given situation. This thought process may be cyclical and self-fulfilling, but in most cases, the belief is wholly erroneous and has been significantly exaggerated in the person's mind.

Low motivation. Most people will, at times, experience low motivation: that feeling of having very little to begin or continue with a task. For people with dyslexia, this can be particularly pronounced as the stress, energy and concentration can in time lead to exhaustion and significant dips in enthusiasm to continue.

Dyspraxia

What is dyspraxia?

Like dyslexia, dyspraxia is a specific learning difficulty (SpLD) that can affect individuals throughout their lives (Cantell et al., 1994; Cousins and Smyth, 2003; Dyspraxia Foundation, 2021; Hill and Brown 2013). It is estimated to affect 5%–10% of the population (Zwicker et al., 2013; Harries et al., 2015) and is 'characterized by marked impairment of motor coordination that substantially interferes with an individual's academic achievement and/or activities of daily living' (Hunt et al., 2021: 562).

Dyspraxia is an immaturity or delay in motor control which can affect an individual's ability to plan future acts, process information or instructions sequentially, and is associated with problems related to cognition and language development. Although there is no cure for dyspraxia, and its causes are likewise shrouded in uncertainty, the American Psychiatric Association's latest edition of the Diagnostic and Statistical Manual of Mental Disorders (DSM-5) categorises it as a 'learning disorder' and subcategorises it as a "neurodevelopmental" motor disorder. What this essentially means is that a dyspraxic individual's motor delay and coordination difficulties are caused by signals and messages not being fully transmitted by the brain. In this respect, dyspraxia should be understood as a mental processing difficulty that has a direct effect on physical coordination and adversely affects a person's ability to develop motor skills.

Characteristics of dyspraxia

Gross motor coordination

- Poor or reduced movement, coordination and balance.
- Underdeveloped hand-eye coordination.
- Exaggerated gestures (gesticulation).
- Propensity to appear clumsy.

Fine motor coordination

General characteristics

Poor handling/manipulative skills. Difficulty grasping small objects, manipulating tools or equipment. There may also be some inconsistency when using new or specialist equipment.

Manual dexterity. It has been noted that in some people with dyspraxia, hand dominance may be poorly established, thereby affecting activities such as dressing and cleaning, as well taking part in sporting activities.

Difficulties writing, typing or notetaking. If students with dyspraxia are expected to take notes during teaching sessions, there is a likelihood that the quality of their writing will decline. Their handwriting speed will be much lower than average, meaning that accurate transcription of session will not be possible.

Students may not be able to complete written exams on time, even if they are provided with the use of a computer. Writing speeds will vary between individuals, so adjustments will depend on respective strengths and abilities.

Impact on learning

Information processing difficulties. Information processing difficulties makes it hard for people to automatically process what others are saying. Their ability to discern the subtle differences between units of sound will not be strong, meaning that there is a possibility of mishearing or misunderstanding what has been said. Difficulties can be exacerbated in noisy environments or when two or more people are speaking at once. In such circumstances, dyspraxic students may struggle to understand instructions or forget key elements of what has been said.

Reduced/difficulty with cognition (executive functioning). Executive dysfunction covers a variety of cognitive, psychological and behavioural issues that are associated with SpLD. People may experience difficulties with personal organisation and planning, being organised or meeting deadlines. Goal-oriented tasks are often compromised because of executive dysfunction, meaning that preparing for future events such as deadlines or group work objectives will be difficult.

Difficulty following instructions and multi-tasking. If dyspraxic students are working on several assignments or tasks at once, then progress could be limited. They are likely to struggle throughout the term or whole year, with things only getting worse as deadlines approach. If additional advice and guidance is provided, then it should be responsive to their overall cognitive profile and learning style. In practice, this may mean extending deadlines for some assignments, providing technique for overcoming procrastination and working towards smaller, goal-oriented tasks.

What is ADHD?

ADHD is an acronym for attention deficit hyperactivity disorder, which as the name suggests is a condition that mainly presents behaviourally, particularly in relation to a person being mostly hyperactive or mostly inattentive or mostly impulsive. ADHD is often identified in childhood and is initially based on observations of a child's behaviour. Specifically, a child's difficulty managing certain behaviours such as being unable to pay attention, sitting still and concentrating, controlling impulsive behaviours and excessive fidgeting and talking. As the child progresses into adulthood, the main symptoms of ADHD may diminish as the individual matures sufficiently to control their behaviour. However, ADHD is a lifelong condition, which means that many adults will continue to experience problems with work, homelife or relationships to varying degrees (ADHD Foundation, 2021; Centre for Disease Control and Prevention, 2021).

The table on next page, from DSM-5 (American Psychological Association, 2021) symptoms, breaks down the main characteristics of the condition, locating each sub-set symptom as being consistent with inattentiveness, hyperactive-impulsive or a combination.

Although a list of symptoms can be a useful tool for conveying the primary traits of ADHD, it is the impact the condition has on the lived experience that should be equally emphasised. Of course, this is not so easily done, so will require opportunities to be provided for students to discuss how they have lived with their ADHD, how well they are managing their condition and what the main risk factors are regarding associated problems with mental health

Presentations	Symptoms
Inattentive	Most or all of the following symptoms, excluding situations where these symptoms are better explained by another psychiatric or medical condition: • Be easily distracted, miss details, forget things and frequently switch from one activity to another • Have difficulty maintaining focus on one task • Become bored with a task after only a few minutes, unless doing something they find enjoyable • Have difficulty focusing attention on organising or completing a task • Have trouble completing or turning in homework assignments, often losing things (e.g., pencils, toys, assignments) needed to complete tasks or activities • Appear not to be listening when spoken to • Daydream, become easily confused, and move slowly • Have difficulty processing information as quickly and accurately as others • Struggle to follow instructions • Have trouble understanding details; overlooks details
Hyperactive-impulsive	Most or all of the following symptoms, excluding situations where these symptoms are better explained by another psychiatric or medical condition: • Fidget or squirm a great deal • Talk nonstop • Dash around, touching or playing with anything and everything in sight • Have trouble sitting still during dinner, school and while doing homework • Be constantly in motion • Have difficulty performing quiet tasks or activities • Be impatient • Blurt out inappropriate comments, show their emotions without restraint and act without regard for consequences • Have difficulty waiting for things they want or waiting their turn in games • Often interrupt conversations or others' activities
Combined	Meet the criteria for both inattentive and hyperactive-impulsive ADHD.

and learning development. This is because unlike dyslexia and dyspraxia, the 'secondary symptoms' such as anxiety, depression and stress are reportedly more severe, with the charity Mind stating that there is evidence 'anxiety, depression, conduct disorder (persistent patterns of antisocial, aggressive or defiant behaviour), substance abuse, and sleep problems are all more common with people who have ADHD' (Mind, 2021). The stresses that come from living with ADHD were illustrated by historian Dr Kate Lister who explained that the traits of inattentiveness and hyperactivity are more connected than one would immediately realise as the former often influences behaviour leading to the latter:

> Despite the name, attention is not something an ADHD brain is deficient in. What the brain struggles to do is to regulate attention. Whereas a neurotypical brain can filter out and then prioritise various stimuli, the ADHD brain can't, which means it will try and focus on everything equally, or it will focus attention on the wrong thing.
>
> (Lister, 2020)

Of particular interest is her description of the effects prescription medication had to manage and regulate her symptoms of ADHD. 'I had no idea how 'noisy' my brain was until I started taking ADHD medication, and to begin with, the silence absolutely terrified me. Without the constant mental chatter, days seemed to drag on for weeks, I felt lonely…' (Lister, 2020). As we can see, diagnosis, support and medical treatment will not necessarily mean that the symptoms have been wholly mitigated. For this reason, it is important to point out that while medication plays an important part in the overall support for people with ADHD, it is not a cure in pill form for what is in reality a highly complex neurodevelopmental issue. Thus, while the most pronounced symptoms of dyslexia and dyspraxia can be ameliorated somewhat through certain pedagogic interventions, ADHD's unique difference is that prescriptive medication for many is often integral to the management of the condition, along with cognitive, emotional or behavioural therapy.

Medication

All treatment for ADHD, whether therapy or medicine, can help lessen the symptoms, but only to the extent that an individual can better manage to function. Prescriptive medication is not, therefore, 'a permanent cure for ADHD but may help someone with the condition concentrate better, be less impulsive, feel calmer, and learn and practise new skills' (NHS, 2021). The caveat here is that, as Dr Kate Lister explained, the abrupt change in cognitive functioning can have an equally dramatic effects on the person.

In the UK, there are five types of medicine licensed for the treatment of ADHD. The following information, from NHS UK, breaks down the five licensed medicines, along with possible side effects. When supporting students with ADHD, it is important that consideration is given to the likely impact the drugs may have on the individual's sense of self and the feelings they evoke. These are pharmaceutical interventions intended to regulate not just concentration but behaviour also. Sudden personality changes may need to be monitored.

Specific learning difficulties (SpLD) 21

Drug	Description	Possible side effects
Methylphenidate	Methylphenidate is the most commonly used medicine for ADHD. It belongs to a group of medicines called stimulants, which work by increasing activity in the brain, particularly in areas that play a part in controlling attention and behaviour. Methylphenidate may be offered to adults, teenagers and children over the age of 5 with ADHD. The medicine can be taken as either immediate-release tablets (small doses taken two to three times a day) or as modified-release tablets (taken once a day in the morning, with the dose released throughout the day).	• a small increase in blood pressure and heart rate • loss of appetite, which can lead to weight loss or poor weight gain • trouble sleeping • headaches • stomach aches • mood swings
Lisdexamfetamine	Lisdexamfetamine is a medicine that stimulates certain parts of the brain. It improves concentration, helps focus attention and reduces impulsive behaviour. It may be offered to teenagers and children over the age of 5 with ADHD if at least six weeks of treatment with methylphenidate has not helped. Adults may be offered lisdexamfetamine as the first-choice medicine instead of methylphenidate. Lisdexamfetamine comes in capsule form, taken once a day.	• decreased appetite, which can lead to weight loss or poor weight gain • aggression • drowsiness • dizziness • headaches • diarrhoea • nausea and vomiting
Dexamfetamine	Dexamfetamine is similar to lisdexamfetamine and works in the same way. It may be offered to adults, teenagers and children over the age of 5 with ADHD. Dexamfetamine is usually taken as a tablet once or twice a day, although an oral solution is also available.	• decreased appetite • mood swings • agitation and aggression • dizziness • headaches • diarrhoea • nausea and vomiting

(Continued)

22 Specific learning difficulties (SpLD)

Drug	Description	Possible side effects
Atomoxetine	Atomoxetine works differently from other ADHD medicines. It's a selective noradrenaline reuptake inhibitor (SNRI), which means it increases the amount of a chemical in the brain called noradrenaline. This chemical passes messages between brain cells, and increasing it can aid concentration and help control impulses. Atomoxetine may be offered to adults, teenagers and children over the age of 5 if it's not possible to use methylphenidate or lisdexamfetamine. It's also licensed for use in adults if symptoms of ADHD are confirmed. Atomoxetine comes in capsule form, usually taken once or twice a day. Atomoxetine has also been linked to some more serious side effects that are important to look out for, including suicidal thoughts and liver damage.	• a small increase in blood pressure and heart rate • nausea and vomiting • stomach aches • trouble sleeping • dizziness • headaches • irritability
Guanfacine	Guanfacine acts on part of the brain to improve attention, and it also reduces blood pressure. It may be offered to teenagers and children over the age of 5 if it's not possible to use methylphenidate or lisdexamfetamine. Guanfacine should not be offered to adults with ADHD. Guanfacine is usually taken as a tablet once a day, in the morning or evening.	• tiredness or fatigue • headache • abdominal pain • dry mouth

What is autism?

Case study – Rachael

Rachael arrived at university hoping to study natural sciences. This would be her first time away from home as she had decided to live in student accommodation. She had already informed the university that she had autism and ADHD, was taking medication to control her impulsive behaviour and would require support to help her academically. Her academic adjustments were recommended and put in place as soon as she registered on her degree. On top of the additional time for exams, she was allowed to take them in a private room, was given rest breaks and it had been arranged for her to sit examinations in the afternoons. Her disability services arranged to meet her regularly along with her personal tutor to make sure she was transitioning into university well and coping with the abrupt chance of lifestyle. During these meetings, it soon become evidence that Rachael was struggling in her accommodation and focussing on teaching sessions. She was not used to being around so many people for so long. In her accommodation, she was finding it difficult to cope with noises that came from late-night activities, while in lectures, the sounds of so many other people in large lecture theatres caused her to experience intense anxieties. Working with the accommodation office, it was arranged for Rachael to be moved to another accommodation block, one mostly used by mature students and postgraduates. Although this did not stop late-night noises, it minimised them enough for her to feel more comfortable. Her support plan was amended also to include recommendations for sympathy to be given if her attendance fluctuates. There were times when Rachael needed to simply leave the room, go to a quiet place on campus and calm herself until she felt able enough to return.

Autism

Of the conditions covered so far, autism is perhaps the one that defies categorisation the most. One reason is that as with the prevalence of comorbidity between dyslexia and dyspraxia, so too with ADHD and autism. Both conditions coexist at very high rates, with both similarly having symptoms that resemble each other in marked ways, with some researchers suggesting that autism and ADHD coexist at levels between 20% and 37% (Lai et al., 2014; Hollingdale et al., 2019).

Another factor adding to the uncertainty of 'what' autism is, is the rather fluid and changing nature of its many definitions and descriptions. NHS UK, for example, makes the point that autism has different names for many people, with terms such as autism spectrum disorder (ASD), autism spectrum condition (ASC) and Asperger's (or Asperger syndrome) being 'used by some people to describe autistic people with average or above average intelligence' (NHS, 2021). The medical classification of autism, particularly DSM-5's, is similarly replete with multiple sub-categorisation, with Cullen pointing out that 'the classification of ADSs now encompass disorders such as autism disorder, Asperger's disorder and pervasive development disorder … and include those individuals with symptoms such as "deficits in social communication" and "restrictive, repetitive patterns of behaviour"' (Cullen, 2015: 90). Previously, Asperger's syndrome was classified in the earlier DSM-4 edition as a condition separate from autism, chiefly on account of the presentation of symptoms being less severe than 'classic' autism traits. For example, those with the condition were said to have high cognitive functioning and language skills equal to neurotypical people (Autism Society, 2021). As Asperger's syndrome in particular has been subsumed into the DSM-5 broader understanding of autism, we need to be sensitive to the self-identification that invariably comes with diagnostic labelling. In other words, it does not inevitably follow that just because Asperger's syndrome is autism that people with Asperger's will see themselves as autistic. The National Autistic Society rightly states that each person

> is different, and it is up to each individual how they choose to identify. Some people with a diagnosis of Asperger syndrome may choose to keep using the term, while others may prefer to refer to themselves as autistic or on the autistic spectrum.
> (National Autistic Society, 2021)

As with other learning difficulties, autistic individuals experience extremely high levels of mental health issues, with depression, anxiety and stress being particularly evident.

What sort of support and adjustments an autistic student requires at university will depend on the severity of the condition and the potential for disablement to occur within an unadjusted environment. Autism must necessarily be seen as a condition that extends beyond its impact on learning development, and one in which 'care for people with autism needs to be accompanied by actions at community and societal levels' (WHO, 2021).

The chief characteristics of dyslexia and dyspraxia are primarily located within an educational context, with the proviso that associated symptoms of stress and anxiety may also be present. However, with autism and to a similar extent ADHD, the notion that either can be similarly contextualised is not so straight forward. It is a condition that affects how people communicate and interact with the world (NAS, 2021), but 'there is great variation in how individuals are affected' (Boyd et al., 2011). Much attention on autism has focused as much on social context as it has on the educational implications. This means for universities the emphasis should focus on adjustments intended to make the environment as a whole inclusive and supportive. And one such occasion when this is expected to occur is during the transition from school/college to higher education. For many autistic people, it is often the case that changes to established routines or a sudden disruption to the familiar can be difficult, often to the point that when facing challenges such as student life and daily independent living there is a major impact on their wellbeing (Van Hees et al., 2015). Transitioning into a higher education setting has the potential to cause considerable problems for an autistic student. Generally, most students' initial experiences of higher education are social and not educational, with introduction weeks comprising of social activities, induction and welcome events that take up the bulk of their time. For some autistic individuals, their primary difficulties may lie with peer interaction and social communication rather than academic and educational development (Cullen, 2015).

Cai and Richdale's (2016) have identified four themes most likely to affect an autistic student's experiences of university:

- comorbid conditions – other SpLDs, mental health or health-related difficulties.
- transition – their research indicated that transition into university was often unplanned, therefore detrimental.
- disclosure – this is a particular problem for those who choose to disclose their autism diagnosis after enrolment and after problems begin to occur.
- service and support – autistic students often felt more educationally supported than socially supported.

Cai and Richdale reinforce similar findings by Adreon, D. and Durocher, J.S. (2007). Adreon and Durcher (2007) who also concluded that autistic students transitioning into higher education were 'likely to experience significant and unique challenges in adjusting to postsecondary education', specifically socialisation, communication, independent daily living, academic functioning and self-advocacy.

The National Autistic Society identifies six key area of difficulty most likely to be experienced by autistic people. The following is a summary of the main areas.

Social communication and social interaction challenges. Autistic individuals can sometimes have difficulty interpreting verbal and non-verbal language (oral communication and body language).

Although speech and language communication may be problematic, this does not mean that autistic people lack the capacity to experience the same thoughts, feelings and emotions as anyone else. In many instances, the difficulties that arise from being able to express their internal selves can lead to frustrations and feelings of disempowerment. This can be especially difficult if the person lacks the ability to fully understand abstract concepts or the nuances of conversation, e.g. sarcasm and ironic phrases.

Repetitive and restrictive behaviour. For some autistic people, social conventions may seem impossibly difficult to grasp as many of the rules that govern the social self are unwritten and governed by mutually agreed yet unspecified codes of conduct.

Holding to routine or repetitive behaviour allows the individual to establish a feeling of control, which in an environment otherwise beset by the unpredictable and uncertainty can serve as a surrogate for certainty and order.

A change of circumstances or disruption to routine can provoke distressing reactions that can lead to high levels of anxiety and mental health problems.

Under or over-sensitivity to light, sounds, taste or touch. Some autistic individuals are hypersensitive, which means they are acutely sensitive and find uncomfortable feeling, hearing, seeing or touching certain things, lights or smells.

Highly focused interests or hobbies. Although this may change over time, many children who develop highly focused interests may carry this through to adulthood. A positive aspect of this side of autism is that the intense focus that comes with this symptom can lead to highly productive academic progress. However, another aspect is that, like ADHD, the student may equally focus on important and not so unimportant areas of their work.

Extreme anxiety. According to the NAS, over a third of autistic people experience serious mental health issues. As many autistic individuals find it extremely difficult regulating their emotions and participating in social activities, the toll this can take emotionally and psychologically can lead to debilitating mental health and physical problems.

Meltdowns and shutdowns. If an autistic person becomes overwhelmed with a situation, they may lose behavioural control (e.g. lose tempter, become uncommunicative). Meltdowns may involve stimming (self-stimulatory behaviour such as repetitively gesturing, rocking, extreme fidgeting).

Barriers to learning

Physical spaces

Orientation: Consideration should be given to the affect a new physical environment may have on someone with poor short-term memory, information processing difficulties, reduced spatial awareness and/or heightened sensitivity to their sensory surroundings.

Consider the following procedural adjustments:

- Provide all students with disabilities the opportunity to disclose their diagnoses as early as the application stage.
- As well as open day events, provide individuals with the opportunity for personalised orientation days. For students with limited spatial awareness

or those who experience adverse reactions to abrupt changes in their lives and new physical surroundings, this helps familiarise the layout of the campus.
- Make available campus maps and if feasible links to online virtual campus tours.

Sensory factors

- **Background noise, smells and other sensory distractions:** As well as using orientation days to become more familiar with the campus, also work with the student to determine what, if any, sensory distractions may be present. This can be categorised into the following:

Location	Cause	Adjustment
Campus/ surrounding area	• **Sounds:** traffic, cleaning equipment and electric motors, music through speaker systems, emergency vehicle sirens, people talking in large groups/social gatherings, murmuring, planes flying overhead, keyboard tapping, telephone ring tones, fire alarms, ventilation/air con systems. • **Smells:** cleaning products, perfumes, snacks and drinks, unventilated rooms.	• Anticipate and identify potential causes of auditory discomfort – are fire alarm drills scheduled to be at regular times? Do cleaning staff have a schedule for using certain types of electric equipment on particular days and in specific locations? Is the campus near a main road or airport? It may not be possible or realistic to compile a comprehensive audit of potentially unsettling sounds across the whole of the campus, but this should not prevent staff from being aware of the main background noises that could contribute to auditory discomfort. • Establish a dialogue with the student; identify which auditory experiences they perceive to be painful, disruptive or intense. These may be background and impossible to mitigate. • Advise students that campus premises are cleaned regularly, and that the aroma of certain cleaning products will be stronger at some times.

(Continued)

Location	Cause	Adjustment
Teaching spaces	• **Sounds**: ventilation/air con units; electrical devices, group discussions, coughing/sneezing, keyboard tapping, whispering/quietly talking. • **Smells**: other students, perfumes, deodorants, snacks/drinks.	• Allow students to be flexible with their attendance. Sensory overload caused by environmental triggers is not conducive to learning, so if the physical space is causing such a detrimental effect, then allow the student to remove themselves. • It may be necessary to switch off some devices such as air conditioning units, fans or other electrical devices. • If the triggering noises come from outside, then close windows and doors. This may be problematic at certain times of the year. • If possible, keep the room temperature at an ambient level. Heat or cold sensitivity can impact on autistic students quite severely. • Allow for some autistic students to wear sound inhibitors such as earplugs or headphones. • During group discussions, encourage respectful interactions amongst all students – one speaker at a time, repeat questions and summarise points if ambiguously phrased.
Accommodation/social spaces	• **Sounds**: other students' daily living (cooking, washing, etc.), late-night activities (parties, socialising); cleaners and maintenance staff; doors slamming, talking loudly, music (either too loud or muffled yet audible). • **Smells**: other students' food; shared bathrooms or toilet facilities.	It would not be reasonable to impose adjustments on other students. However, this does not mean that discussions cannot be held between students in shared accommodation or hall of residence. If possible, encourage meetings that include resident or hall mentors and students, discuss what the implications are of environmental sensitivity. If the student accommodation ultimately proves to be disabling and too much, then this might need to be anticipated beforehand. Contracts should reflect this and include some caveats to allow students to remove themselves from their accommodation with no financial sanctions.

Teaching, learning and assessment

Pre-registration

Marketing and recruitment have a responsibility to communicate what support and advice services are available to SpLD and disabled students. Websites and promotional material should provide information about how students can access internally available support services, along with contact details of relevant departments. Information for applicant students necessarily needs to be accessible; this will involve using clear, unambiguous language in all material and correspondence. This is especially important if the course requires some form of pre-registration assessment or test.

Quality assurance issues will also need to be addressed with applicant students. Many courses are externally accredited which means some negotiation may be required for certain adjustments. For example, if a student should require exam papers reformatted and re-worded to include unambiguous language, then it should be made clear whether the accrediting organisation will need to be contacted for their approval. For academic, support and administrative staff, knowing what the procedure is for adjustments to an accredited degree assessment procedure is vital to ensure students are not disadvantaged or unnecessarily inconvenienced.

Routes of entry to HE should be made available to academic staff. It is probable that academic staff will receive individual learning support plans at some point, but these plans may only contain limited information about students' disabilities. SpLDs can affect students differently depending on their personal circumstances, age, access or otherwise to previous support. For tutors to know whether access to students' degree was via traditional A levels, Highers, BTECs or Access courses will furnish their understanding of students' past educational experiences and possibly help manage expectations.

Pre-entry events scheduled into the institution's calendar are an excellent way for SpLD/disabled students to visit the campus along with their parents/ guardians, school/college support and transition workers. Ideally, these events are in addition to open days and individual orientation visits, so should endeavour to include other institutional staff, including support staff from other non-disability services (counselling, learning development/study skills, finance advice, accommodation, peer mentors, etc.) and academic staff. As many SpLD students will have or are considering applying for additional funding for specialist support, consideration should be given to also including representatives of local assessment centres and external providers of specialist student support. The purpose of these visits is to introduce students and their wider support network to the campus life and higher education, as well as give all visitors a chance to ask questions and follow-up queries.

Pre-enrolment support plans should be drafted and completed in the weeks and months leading up to the start of term. Including the student in the initial drafting and completion of the plans allows for a line of communication to be established that will hopefully minimise the amount of time they would otherwise spend self-advocating after their arrival at the institution. The language contained within the plans needs to be concise and unambiguous, with the focus as much a possible away from a deficit model of disability. The plan itself is intended for both students and staff as a reference point upon which agreed adjustments and respective responsibilities are based. To that end, in addition to recommendations for adjustments, the plan can also include the following:

1. Student's preferred method of communication (e.g. email, phone).
2. Course requirements – main teaching and learning methods (lectures, seminars, group activities, presentations and independent study).
3. Information on accessing appropriate support aligned with course requirements – study skills advice for essay writing, library services for independent study and counselling services for dealing with work-related anxiety and stress.

Accommodation visits, especially during the summer, can be excellent ways for SpLD students to familiarise themselves with student life. This would also be an ideal time to introduce applicant students to peer mentors to discuss the realities of daily independent living.

During induction/fresher's week, some students may struggle in crowds or become agitated in new surroundings. While experiencing information processing difficulties, they may find participation problematic. To minimise any problems, and to adjust such occasions to make them more accessible for SpLD students, the following is recommended:

1. Provide a detailed breakdown of what they should expect in terms of scheduled activities, locations and expected levels of participation.
2. Students with SpLD need to be made aware in advance who the ambassadors/mentors are, what their roles are and how they can be approached.
3. Many universities recruit student ambassadors and/or peer mentors of some description. Ideally, SpLD students should have allocated (if they choose) a buddy or mentor to help them navigate their way through their initial experiences. If this is not feasible, then ambassadors and mentors need to be alerted to the likelihood that some SpLD students may need advice finding their way around the campus to specific locations, understanding their timetables or finding resources.
4. Students should also be reassured that during the first few weeks of a new term, it is not uncommon for timetables to change at short notice. Also, further reassurances should be made that any late arrivals or missed sessions will not result in penalties.

Teaching and learning

There are several anticipatory measures that can be adopted by academic staff to begin the process of ensuring their teaching and learning environments are inclusive for SpLD students.

Firstly, recognise that all classes will contain students with a huge variety of learning styles, literacy difficulties and degrees of information processing ability. Not all students will take on board what is taught at the same rate or indeed in the same way.

Course design

SpLD challenges	Reasonable adjustments
Dyslexia/dyspraxia • Literacy and language skills • Working memory • Time management • Processing speed ADHD • Inattentiveness • Hyperactive/impulsive • Medication side effect Autism • Social communication and interaction • Sensory overload • Repetitive behaviour • Shutdown/meltdown	• Make available a course overview or 'road-map' for the module or whole course. • Be very clear about the learning outcomes of the course/module. Inform students what they should know, understand or be able to demonstrate by the end of their programme. Be sure to clearly differentiate between learning outcomes and module/programme aims, which can be understood to mean a concise overview of the purpose of the course. • It is important to ensure that any course or module description communicates learning outcomes that are tutor focussed and student focussed – i.e., be clear how the tutor plans to achieve the aims of the programme, and how students will demonstrate their learning. • Incorporate formative assessments into the programme, keeping in mind that some students may have preferred methods of communication, varying levels of concentration and information processing levels. • Provide a glossary of specialist terms. • Be clear from the beginning why certain teaching and learning techniques will be used (e.g., lectures, discussion, group work) and how they are aligned with the learning outcomes and assessment procedures.

(Continued)

Specific learning difficulties (SpLD)

SpLD challenges	Reasonable adjustments
	• Build assessment flexibility into the course; if alternative assessment procedures are required, consider what would and would not be reasonable or unreasonable; Q: does the recommended alternative assessment undermine the academic integrity of the course? Can the learning outcomes still be demonstrated? • Ensure any alternative assessments do not place disabled/SpLD students at a disadvantage. • Provide a thorough reading list, aligning key texts to weekly lecture schedule and highlighting core reading with background material.

Course delivery

SpLD challenges	Reasonable adjustments
Dyslexia/dyspraxia • Literacy and language skills • Working memory • Processing speed ADHD • Inattentiveness • Hyperactive/impulsive • Medication side effect Autism • Social communication and interaction • Sensory overload • Repetitive behaviour • Shutdown/meltdown	• Include a variety of multisensory teaching strategies; audio/visual aids. • Allow for missed sessions to be available online or provide opportunities for catch-up sessions. • State learning outcomes at the outset of each teaching session. • Provide a session overview of structure, main points to be covered, intended teaching and learning activities. • Be clear to students the extent to which they may be expected to participate, e.g., voluntary Q&As, group work. • If necessary, make adjustments to group work: agree ground rules and expectations, assign group members and roles where necessary and monitor progress. • Assume some students will record sessions; therefore, make clear if the lecture/seminar will be recorded and made available on the VLE.

SpLD challenges	Reasonable adjustments
	• Lecture materials in advance: ensure teaching materials are made available via the VLE with at least 24 hours in advance. • Reassure students that permission does not need to be sought if they need to leave the session. • Some students may require note takers to sit with them in the session. Work with the student and/or their note taker to inform them in advance what the session's aims are, and if possible, to provide them in advance with lecture notes and a glossary of key terms. Provide opportunities for note takers to ask for clarification. • Notify students (and note takers) of any planned change to the timetable, e.g., different time or location. Reassure students there will be no penalties if this disruption may result in the session being missed. • Students should not be asked to read aloud or contribute to discussions without advance warning.

Accessing resources

SpLD challenges	Reasonable adjustments
<u>Dyslexia/dyspraxia</u> • Literacy and language skills • Working memory • Processing speed <u>ADHD</u> • Inattentiveness • Hyperactive/impulsive • Medication side effect <u>Autism</u> • Social communication and interaction • Sensory overload • Repetitive behaviour • Shutdown/meltdown	• The library: contact details of subject librarians to be provided. • Include as part of initial induction, navigation of the physical space, location of key texts in the library, booking out systems and library gateways. • Extensions on all library loans and/or equipment. • Be aware of any study rooms or quiet spaces students may go to if over stimulated.

(Continued)

34 Specific learning difficulties (SpLD)

SpLD challenges	Reasonable adjustments
	• For practical courses, provide students with opportunities to familiarise themselves with unfamiliar equipment. This will benefit students with motor coordination difficulties or who may experience anxiety about using new devices. • If necessary, provide additional informal or formal sessions for students to familiarise themselves with specialist or course equipment. • Some students may initially require detailed written instructions explaining how some devices or equipment should be used. If you create a document detailing how devices are to be used, consider the following: whether illustrations need to be included; avoiding ambiguous or unclear language; whether using a device needs to follow sequential operations; how the equipment relates to other devices (e.g., for some media courses, camera operations will relate to lighting and sound mixing).

Assessments (accessible/alternative)

SpLD challenges	Reasonable adjustments
<u>Dyslexia/dyspraxia</u> • Literacy and language skills • Working memory • Processing speed <u>ADHD</u> • Inattentiveness • Hyperactive/impulsive • Medication side effect <u>Autism</u> • Social communication and interaction • Sensory overload • Repetitive behaviour • Shutdown/meltdown	<u>Coursework</u> • Ensure all students are clear about the institution's policy on deadlines; i.e., whether or not automatic extensions can be granted as a reasonable adjustment. • Be clear to students very early how they may apply for deadline extensions (depending on respective intuitional policy).

SpLD challenges	Reasonable adjustments
	• Students will need to understand at the start of their programme the process for applying for mitigating circumstances, i.e., what can and cannot be accepted as mitigation; what evidence should be provided; what the process involves. • Be aware if possible whether the student has access to specialist external support; this can be 1:1 study skills advice or mentoring, for example. If the support relates to developing academic skills and overcoming SpLD barriers to learning, provide an opportunity to discuss with students what skills they need to develop as they relate to the learning outcomes and assessment criteria. • If the institution has an in-house learning development or study advice service, make this known to all students. This should especially be done during the formative, monitoring process during the term. Exams • Additional time – 25% • Rest breaks – not to be included as part of the 25% extra time • Room on own • Smaller room with fewer students • Choice of seating – e.g., near the exit, at the back, at the front • Scribe Alternative assessments • Include alternative assessments into the course design; if a disabled/SpLD student requires or is recommended alternative assessments, be clear what their possible choices are. • Alternative assessments should be aligned with the learning outcomes; the student should be neither advantaged nor disadvantaged.

(Continued)

SpLD challenges	Reasonable adjustments
	• Build into the programme a process for students to request alternative assessments, with the choice of alternatives already provided. • If some alternative assessments are not possible, then this should be communicated as early as possible and followed up with a focus on supporting the student to develop the necessary skills to take part in the assessment process.

References

ADHD Foundation. (2021). https://www.adhdfoundation.org.uk/

Adreon, D. and Durocher, J.S. (2007). Evaluating the college transition needs of individuals with high-functioning autism spectrum disorders. *Intervention in School and Clinic*, 42(5), pp. 271–279.

American Psychiatric Association. (2013). *Diagnostic and statistical manual of mental disorders*. 5th edition. American Psychiatric Publishing.

American Psychiatric Association (2013) *Diagnostic and statistical manual of mental disorders: DSM-5*. 5th edn. Washington, DC: American Psychiatric Publishing.

American Psychological Association. (2021). https://www.apa.org/topics/adhd

Autism Society. (2021). Asperger's Syndrome. https://www.autism-society.org/what-is/aspergers-syndrome/

Boyd, K., Woodbury-Smith, M. and Szatmari, P. (2011). Managing anxiety and depressive symptoms in adults with autism-spectrum disorders. *Journal of Psychiatry and Neuroscience*, 36(4), pp. E35–E36.

British Dyslexia Association. (2021). 'What is Dyslexia?' https://www.bdadyslexia.org.uk/dyslexia/about-dyslexia/what-is-dyslexia#:~:text=Dyslexia%20is%20a%20learning%20difficulty,is%20actually%20about%20information%20processing.

Cai, R.Y. and Richdale, A.L. (2016). Educational experiences and needs of higher education students with autism spectrum disorder. *Journal of Autism and Developmental Disorders*, 46, pp. 31–41.

Cantell, M.H., Smyth, M.M. and Ahonen, T.P. (1994). Clumsiness in adolescence: Educational, motor, and social outcomes of motor delay detected at 5 years. *Adapted Physical Activity Quarterly*, 11, pp. 115–129.

Carroll, J.M. and Iles, J.E. (2006). An assessment of anxiety levels in dyslexic students in higher education. *British Journal of Educational Psychology*, 76, pp. 651–662.

Centres for Disease Control and Prevention. (2021). https://www.cdc.gov/

Cousins, M. and Smyth, M.M. (2003). Developmental coordination impairments in adulthood. *Human Movement Science*, 22, pp. 433–459.

Cullen, J.A. (2015). The needs of college students with autism spectrum disorders and Asperger's Syndrome. *Journal of Postsecondary Education and Disability*, 28(1), pp. 89–101.

Dyspraxia Foundation. (2021). https://dyspraxiafoundation.org.uk/

Fiorello, C.A., Hale, J.B. and Snyder, L.E. (2006). Cognitive hypothesis testing and response to intervention for children with reading problems. *Psychology in the Schools*, 43(8), pp. 835–853.

Hill, E.L. and Brown, D. (2013). Mood impairments in adults previously diagnosed with developmental coordination disorder. *Journal of Mental Health*, 22, pp. 334–340.

Hollingdale, J., Woodhouse, E., Young, S., Fridman, A. and Mandy, W. (2019). Autistic spectrum disorder symptoms in children and adolescents with attention deficit/hyperactivity disorder: A meta-analytical review. *Psychological Medicine, BMC Psychiatry*, 19, p. 404.

Hunt, J., Zwicker, J.G., Godecke, E. and Raynor, A. (2021). Awareness and knowledge of developmental coordination disorder: A survey of caregivers, teachers, allied health professionals and medical professionals in Australia. *Child: Care, Health and Development*. 47(2), pp. 174–183.

International Dyslexia Association. (2021). https://dyslexiaida.org/

Kearns, D.M., Hancock, R., Hoeft, F., Pugh, K.R. and Frost, S.J. (2018). The neurobiology of dyslexia. *Teaching Exceptional Children*, 51(3), pp. 175–188.

Lai, M.C., Lombardo, M.V. and Baron-Cohen, S. (2014). Autism. *The Lancet*, 383(9920), pp. 896–910.

Lister, K. (2020). I was diagnosed with ADHD aged 35 – the biggest hurdle was convincing everyone it's real. iNews. https://inews.co.uk/opinion/adhd-diagnosis-adults-symptoms-treatment-dyslexia-498900.

Mind (website). (2021). ADHD and mental health. https://www.mind.org.uk/information-support/tips-for-everyday-living/adhd-and-mental-health/.

National Autistic Society. (2021). Asperger syndrome and other terms. https://www.autism.org.uk/advice-and-guidance/what-is-autism/asperger-syndrome

NHS (2021). Attention Deficit Hyperactive Disorder https://www.nhs.uk/conditions/attention-deficit-hyperactivity-disorder-adhd/treatment/

Rose, J. (2009). Identifying and teaching children and young people with dyslexia and literacy difficulties: An independent Publisher: Department for Children, Schools and Families.

Shaywitz, S.E. and Shaywitz, B.A. (2008). Paying attention to reading: The neurobiology of reading and dyslexia. *Development and Psychology*, 20, pp. 1329–1349.

Van Hees, V., Moyson, T. and Roeyers, H. (2015). Higher education experiences of students with autism spectrum disorder: Challenges, benefits and support needs. *Journal of Autism and Developmental Disorders*, 45, pp. 1673–1688.

Willcutt, E.G. and Pennington, B.F. (2000). Psychiatric comorbidity in children and adolescents with reading disability. *Journal of Child Psychology and Psychiatry*, 41(8), pp. 1039–1048.

World Health Organisation. (2021). Autism spectrum disorders. https://www.who.int/news-room/fact-sheets/detail/autism-spectrum-disorders

Zwicker, J.G., Harris, S.R. and Klassen, A.F. (2013). Quality of life domains affected in children with developmental coordination disorder: A systematic review. *Child: Care, Health and Development*, 39, pp. 562–580.

Chapter 2

Mental health

Case study – Amy

Amy's university already had in place a robust mental health strategy to support its students. Over the past three years, her institution had recruited several counsellors, cognitive behavioural therapists and wellbeing practitioners as a response to the growing number of students calling for some sort of mental health support presence. In addition to the counselling service, many members of staff, both academic and non-academic, were trained as mental health first aiders. The university had the previous year also amended its mental health policies to include a choice of assessment procedures. Amy began accessing her counselling service towards the end of her first term – as well as the expected stresses that derived from studying at university, she also suffered with long-term post-traumatic stress disorder (PTSD). As her counselling team were employed directly by the university, they were able to liaise with their counterparts in the disability service and academic departments to create a learning plan appropriate for Amy's needs. The insight provided by in-house mental health specialists allowed for many of Amy's issues to be unpacked. For example, while her anxieties intensified in the run up to her assignments' deadline dates, it was recommended that 1:1 academic support be provided by her tutors as additional sessions for her. This enabled Amy to feel more confident in her academic skills, specifically in areas such as assignment writing and using academic language. While her academic tutors were on hand to mitigate against environmental stressors, her counselling service could also provide appropriate therapy to help with the effects of her PTSD. This in time also led to additional adjustments to help with the impact this was having on her work. Recommended reasonable adjustments included allowing a care worker into teaching sessions with her, advance notification of potentially challenging topics during lectures, content warning on reading material and automatic extensions on all assignments.

The impact of depression

Globally, the prevalence of depression is increasing, with the World Health Organization (WHO) estimating that it is 'the single largest contributor of global disability' affecting roughly 3.8% of the world's population (World Health Organization, 2021). The UK higher education sector is not unique in its attempt at responding to the rise in students declaring depression and mental health problems, with Hawkes (2019) declaring that 'university campuses across North America and Europe … are struggling to deal with a rising incidence of mental health problems among students'. Reasonable adjustments in relation to mental health in general and depression in particular must be institutionally responsive and consistent with the mental health strategy of the individual HEI.

Definitions and types of depression

WHO defines depression as categorised by sadness, loss of interest or pleasure, feelings of guilt or low self-worth, disturbed sleep or appetite, feelings of tiredness and poor concentration. Similarly, Mind states that depression 'is a low mood that lasts for a long time, and effects your everyday life', while going on to suggest that at its most severe depression can be life-threatening and can make an individual feel as though everything in life is too hard and less worthwhile. In the UK, the National Institute for Health and Care Excellence (NICE) defines depression in the following way:

The individual must be experiencing five or more symptoms during the same two-week period and at least one of the symptoms should be either (1) depressed mood or (2) loss of interest or pleasure.

1. Depressed mood most of the day, nearly every day.
2. Markedly diminished interest or pleasure in all, or almost all, activities most of the day, nearly every day.
3. Significant weight loss when not dieting or weight gain, or decrease or increase in appetite nearly every day.
4. A slowing down of thought and a reduction of physical movement (observable by others, not merely subjective feelings of restlessness or being slowed down).

5 Fatigue or loss of energy nearly every day.
6 Feelings of worthlessness or excessive or inappropriate guilt nearly every day.
7 Diminished ability to think or concentrate, or indecisiveness, nearly every day.
8 Recurrent thoughts of death, recurrent suicidal ideation without a specific plan or a suicide attempt or a specific plan for committing suicide.

As with other conditions, depression is not without its own sub-categories:

Condition	Definition
Depression	Depression is a low mood that lasts for a long time and affects a person's everyday life. In its mildest form, depression can mean just being in low spirits. It doesn't stop an individual leading a normal life, but it can make everything harder to do and seem less worthwhile. Major depression interferes with an individual's daily life – with eating, sleeping and other everyday activities. Some people may experience only one episode, but it is more common to experience several episodes in a lifetime.
Mild depression	Mild depression is more than a general feeling of being down. Symptoms can last for days or weeks and can affect an individual's daily routine activities. People with mild depression can often manage their symptoms, thereby mitigating their impact on their everyday lives. Mild depression may not be immediately noticeable to most people, but they can still have a debilitating effect on those experiencing the condition.
Moderate depression	In general terms, moderate depression can noticeably impact on an individual's life, particularly their home life, work or studies. Many associated symptoms of moderate depression overlap with mild depression, with the main distinguishing feature being that self-management becomes increasingly difficult to maintain.
Severe depression	Again, symptoms are similar to mild and moderate depression, but are more noticeable to others, and will likely require both a formal diagnosis and substantial intervention. Severe depressive episodes can involve an individual experiencing paranoia, hearing voices, delusions or having suicidal thoughts.
Seasonal affective disorder (SAD)	SAD is a type of depression certain individuals experience during particular times of the year. The symptoms tend to follow the patterns of the seasons or change in weather, leaving the individual feeling in low spirits, lethargic and unmotivated. SAD is often more pronounced during the winter months.

Mental health 41

Condition	Definition
Dysthymia	Dysthymia is a milder form of depression, which is nonetheless long-lasting and quite persistent. According to Harvard Medical School, 'The American Psychiatric Association defines dysthymia as depressed mood most of the time for at least two years, along with at least two of the following symptoms: poor appetite or overeating; insomnia or excessive sleep; low energy or fatigue; low self-esteem; poor concentration or indecisiveness; and hopelessness' (Harvard, 2021). The clinical difference between dysthymia and major depression is that the latter 'may also include two symptoms not found in the standard definition of dysthymia: anhedonia (inability to feel pleasure) and psychomotor symptoms (chiefly lethargy or agitation)' (Harvard, 2021).
Prenatal/ antenatal depression	Depression experienced during pregnancy is called 'prenatal depression'. Most pregnancies experiencing varying degrees of emotion, whether high or low, this is perfectly normal. When feeling low for several days persists with seemingly no alleviation of the mood, then this may be a prenatal depressive episode.
Postnatal depression (PND)	According to NHS, 'Postnatal depression can start any time in the first year after giving birth'. Symptoms of PND might include a persistent low mood, an inability to experience enjoyment or take an interest in anything, fatigue, insomnia, difficulty bonding with the baby and withdrawn. Today, midwives and health visitors are trained to recognise PND. They will have the skills to help guide parents through this difficult time.
Situational depression	Situational depression is a stress-related, short-term category of depression. It may develop after an individual reacts negatively to a traumatic event, making it difficult for them to adjust to everyday living. It is, of course, perfectly understandable for an individual to feel sad, lonely, grief, anxiety or socially isolate themselves following traumatic events, but when these feelings become disproportionate to the event itself, then it may be that situational depression has been triggered.

Anxiety – the mental and physical affects

Anxiety is an emotion characterised by changes in one's physical, psychological and behavioural conditions, usually in the form of feelings of tension and elevated blood pressure, having worried thoughts and experiencing the urge to remove oneself from some situations. Anxiety can also cause irritability and concentration difficulties. For the most part, anxiety is prompted by situations or circumstances that are relatively short-term and manageable. Yet, when anxiety shifts from being a normal emotional state to something considerably more serious is when the physical, emotional and behavioural characteristics escalate in ways that seriously affect a person's everyday life. As a clinical condition, anxiety disorder is an unpleasant emotional state, the cause of which is either unidentified or perceived by the individual to be wholly out of their control and rather disproportionate to their feelings. Individuals with anxiety disorders may experience intrusive thoughts and can prompt changes in their behaviour, for example avoiding or removing themselves from certain situations.

If we take the position that anxiety is a 'future-oriented mood state associated with preparation for possible, upcoming negative events' (Craske et al., 2009; DSM-5), then any institutional response must look at the wider environmental triggers that potentially cause or exacerbate a student's anxious state. In other words, it is more than a condition that exists only in the mind but can be caused directly by the individual's response to environmental pressures. And higher education environments are places almost exclusively geared to preparing students for upcoming events which invariably play a part contributing towards long-term worries. Generally, students tend to be aged between 18 and 24, an age group particularly susceptible to experiencing anxiety, with mentalhealth.org estimating that 'Young people aged 16–24 are more likely to report lower levels of anxiety compared with adults generally', and with students more prone to suffer extremes of anxiety at some point during their studies. What needs unpacking, then, are those elements of anxiety that are chronic and those unadjusted institutional elements that may potentially cause or make worse a very disabling condition.

Categories of anxiety

Anxiety sub-category	Characteristics
Generalised anxiety disorder (GAD)	GAD is the most common anxiety disorder to affect adults. It is characterised by long-term anxiety which is not focused upon anything specific. People who suffer from GAD experience persistent worry and intrusive thoughts and can become disproportionately concerned with everyday matters. 'GAD can cause both psychological (mental) and physical symptoms. These vary from person to person, but can include: • feeling restless or worried • having trouble concentrating or sleeping • dizziness or heart palpitations' (NHS, 2021)

Anxiety sub-category	Characteristics
Panic attacks/disorder	The DSM-5 defines panic attacks as abrupt surges of intense fear or discomfort that peak within minutes. Individuals who experience regular panics are said to have a panic disorder and live in almost constant anticipation of an attack occurring. A panic attack occurs when a person experiences an abrupt sense of fear or terror. Symptoms can include: <ul><li>a racing heartbeat</li><li>feeling faint</li><li>sweating</li><li>nausea</li><li>chest pain</li><li>shortness of breath</li><li>trembling</li><li>hot flushes</li><li>chills</li><li>shaky limbs</li><li>a choking sensation</li><li>dizziness</li><li>numbness or pins and needles</li><li>dry mouth</li><li>a need to go to the toilet</li><li>ringing in your ears</li><li>a feeling of dread or a fear of dying</li><li>a churning stomach</li><li>a tingling in your fingers</li><li>feeling like you're not connected to your body</li></ul>(NHS, 2021)
Social anxiety disorder	Social anxiety disorder is a cognitive, neurological condition that while previously dismissed as 'shyness', is now understood to be chronic and pernicious in nature and has neurobiological underpinnings (Stein and Stein, 2008). People with social anxiety disorder experience anxiety or become fearful of social situations. These can include being introduced to strangers, public speaking and engaging in group discussions or asking for advice and information.

(Continued)

Anxiety sub-category	Characteristics
Post-traumatic stress disorder (PTSD)	PTSD is an anxiety disorder triggered by witnessing or experiencing extremely disturbing or distressing life events. These can include, for example, serious sexual assaults, being the victim of abusive behaviour, being involved in a serious accident or being the victim of a crime. People who have been involved in conflict zones are particularly prone to PTSD. The condition can be disruptive to an individual on a regular or daily basis, with the main symptoms potentially brought about by certain noises, words, phrases, smells or situations. This in turn may cause individuals to avoid particular people, places, situations or events that are likely to remind them of their traumatic experience. The primary symptoms of PTSD differ for each individual, but the condition may present itself in the following ways: Cognitive • difficulty concentrating • lack of interest in recreational or social activities • extreme negative emotions such as guilt or worry • increase in low self-esteem • experience flashbacks to traumatic events Emotional • feelings of disproportionate irritability • agitation • depressed • a sense of numbness, emotionally distant • easily angered by seemingly trivial events Physical • headaches and migraines • high blood pressure • rapidly beating heart rate • dizziness/feeling faint • feeling lightheaded, 'spaced out' • trembling • insomnia

Anxiety sub-category	Characteristics
Health anxiety (hypochondria)	Health anxiety is an anxiety disorder in which a person worries so much about being ill or falling unwell that it becomes an all-consuming distraction in their life. It can develop into an obsessive and irrational concern about developing a serious medical condition, the symptoms of which exist primarily in the individual's imagination. On other occasions, people with health anxiety may misinterpret the symptoms of minor ailments as something more serious. A key feature of health anxiety is a persistent belief that the individual is severely unwell, despite reassurances to the contrary from medical professionals. There is considerable overlap between health anxiety and obsessive-compulsive disorder in that the individual's behaviour and daily life are affected by an obsessional preoccupation with an irritational idea.
Body dysmorphic disorder	Body dysmorphic disorder is an anxiety disorder related to body image. An individual with the condition fixates on one or more perceived flaws in their appearance, these flaws often appearing as quite insignificant or unnoticeable to others. At its most extreme, the condition may prevent a person from going out in public because of the feelings of embarrassment or shame they experience regarding their appearance. People with body dysmorphic disorder fixate on their body image, often repeatedly appraising their reflection, changing their clothes or seeking reassurances about their looks. These repetitive cycles of behaviour may take up a significant proportion of the day, and in time, cause serious distress, while also impacting on the individual's ability to function.
Agoraphobia	Agoraphobia is a category of anxiety disorder whereby a person actively avoids situations or locations that may cause them to feel trapped or confined. The locations themselves can be anything from being in an open space, queuing, commuting on public transport or being in any public space.

(Continued)

Anxiety sub-category	Characteristics
	One of the main symptoms of agoraphobia is the increasing sense of anxiety that comes with the belief that the individual is trapped in a particular place. This symptom is often accompanied by the sense that should anything go wrong then help and assistance would not be available. As well as avoidance strategies, agoraphobia may present in the following ways: • feeling of a loss of control, helplessness • fear that harm or death may occur • breathing problems • sweating and shaking • tight chest/chest pains • feeling sick • unable to focus • panic • a feeling of dread or impending catastrophe • self-consciousness

What is obsessive-compulsive disorder?

Obsessive-compulsive disorder (OCD) is a mental health condition that is estimated to affect between 1% and 3% of the population (National Institute for Health and Care Excellence, 2018). The chief characteristics of OCD are the presence of persistent, unwanted, disturbing thoughts and compulsive, repetitive behaviours. At its most severe, OCD can interfere with an individual's day-to-day life, affect their relationships, employment and domestic lives, which in time can become seriously debilitating. The condition is chronic and long-lasting, and often begins to present during early adulthood.

OCD can cause serious behavioural and functional impairment, and while treatments are available, it must be stressed that those living with the condition may fluctuate in their symptoms depending on their personal circumstances. Symptoms of OCD include a pattern of unwelcome or disturbing thoughts (obsessions) that in their intensity drive certain behaviours (compulsions). Behaviour driven by persistent and troubling thoughts may begin as a means of coping with stresses and anxiety caused by irrational beliefs in certain aspects of a person's life. For example, the notion that someone with OCD cleans either themselves or their home excessively is not necessarily because of their over-commitment to hygiene but because of a fear that not to do so will result in contamination, serious illness and even death. Problems arise when the need to be clean becomes excessive, ritualistic or wholly disproportionate to the perceived threat. Often, however, the link between the obsessive thoughts and compulsive behaviour can be seemingly mundane (checking and rechecking doors are locked) or seemingly more serious with some thoughts driving the belief that the individual will be personally responsible for unrelated future events. Either way, there exists very real issues for people with OCD in that much of their time can be taken up with the rituals and patterns of activities that have no practical benefit or lead to no tangible rewards.

At this point, it is important to note that OCD is not a condition that inevitably leads to delusional beliefs. The DSM-V manual, for instance, stresses that those suffering with OCD are quite likely to be as aware of the irrationality of their actions as anyone, but that their compulsive behaviours are driven by the idea that it is safer to go ahead 'just in case'. There are, according to DSM-V, three distinct levels of insights attributable to OCD:

- Good or fair insight: Characterised by the conscious acknowledgement that obsessive-compulsive beliefs are probably or actually untrue.
- Poor insight: Here people with OCD believe that their obsessive-compulsive beliefs are probably true.
- Absence of insight: Obsessive-compulsive beliefs are absolutely true.

Symptoms of OCD

There are two elements of OCD – obsessions and compulsions. NHS UK also attributes a third element, emotional, which is the associated anxiety and distress that often accompanies a person's unwanted thoughts. But the mental health charity Mind (2021), OCD UK (2021), NICE and the National Institute of Mental Health (2022) all generally agree that OCD is a condition that involves obsessive thoughts and compulsive behaviour.

What exactly is meant by obsessions? These are repeated thoughts, urges or mental images that can cause anxiety or distress. It can also include unwanted sexual or religious thoughts, forbidden or taboo ideas or intrusive and unwanted aggressive thoughts directed towards oneself or others. NHS UK's definition of obsession states that it is 'an unwanted and unpleasant thought, image or urge that repeatedly enters your mind, causing feelings of anxiety, disgust or unease'. For someone with OCD, thoughts come to dominate their thinking to the extent that daily routines and everyday lives are constantly interrupted. Obsessions are differentiated from compulsions by how the person acts upon their thoughts and urges. Visible behavioural signs of OCD can include ordering and arranging items in a particular way, repeatedly checking things such as locked doors or household appliances being switched off or performing less visible mental acts such as counting or repeating certain phrases/mantras. Compulsions are unwanted 'repetitive behaviours or mental acts that the person feels driven to perform' (National Institute for Health and Care Excellence, 2018).

What is bipolar disorder?

Previously known as manic depression, bipolar disorder is a mental health condition that affects mood and behaviour. The condition can cause severe personality swings with individuals experiencing episodes of extreme emotional highs and periods of intense lows. Although it is not unusual for most people to go through periods when their mood or emotional state fluctuates, for individuals experiencing the full onset of bipolar disorder, the symptoms can be distressing and debilitating, with bipolar, according to some researchers, being potentially the deadliest in terms of suicide risk.

The extreme highs and lows of bipolar disorder can be so intense that the condition can feel powerfully overwhelming to the extent that suicidal ideation is commonly reported. The NHS states that 'the risk of suicide for people with bipolar disorder is 15–20 times greater than the general population' (NHS, 2021). Similarly, research by Muller-Oerlinghausen et al. (2002) also states that about '10–20% of individuals with bipolar disorder take their own life, and nearly one third of patients admit to at least one suicide attempt'.

Primary characteristics of bipolar disorder

Manic episodes	- Happy, extreme euphoria - Uncontrollable excitement - Easily distracted, difficulty focusing on one thing at a time - Feeling adventurous, often crossing over to recklessness - Impaired judgement - Concentration problems and difficulty focusing on everyday tasks - Extreme self-confidence – feelings of invulnerability - Self-important, inconsiderate of others - Excessively excited, prolonged feelings of elation **Behavioural symptoms** - Increased energy levels, which over a prolonged period can be physically and mentally unsustainable. The above feelings will invariably present in different ways, but during particularly severe manic episodes, an individual may behave noticeably more friendly, maybe excessively so. As the episode continues, the symptoms may develop into agitation, irritability and rudeness directed against others and may also escalate into aggressive behaviour.

- Another noticeable trait associated with bipolar disorder, and which may be more readily discernible in a higher education environment, is the individual's tendency to be more active socially. This, of course, can mean anything from formal social occasions outside of timetabled daily activities to classroom engagement. Whatever the situation, a manic episode may cause the individual to lose their social inhibitions and behave inappropriately to those around them. Speaking up more frequently during teaching sessions, with speech becoming increasingly rapid and excitable is a symptom that will need to be monitored. Given the potential disruption to the overall learning environment, as well as the adverse effect on the individual's own academic progression, it is incumbent on the HEI to review whether the learning environment is at present fully inclusive for the student.
- Excessive levels of pleasurable but potentially harmful activities; these may include spending money excessively, financially unsustainable gambling, sexual promiscuity or starting projects that are clearly unrealistic in scope. In a similar vein to ADHD, these behaviours can be compulsive and not borne out of any rational forethought. The intention behind the actions is therefore driven more by irrational and sometimes ill-conceived goal orientation rather than a need to alleviate anxiety caused by unwanted/intrusive thoughts.
- Disrupted sleep – sometimes the individual will only manage 2–3 hours of sleep a night. If the manic phase continues for several days, even a week or longer, then the effect upon cognitive functioning will become increasingly pronounced. This will increase the likelihood of the person becoming delusional, experiencing hallucinations and increasingly irrational.

If the individual's delusional thoughts, hallucinations (possibly including hearing voices) and irrational actions continue, then they are at this point experiencing psychosis.

- Psychosis: Psychosis is when a person's perception of reality is at variance with everyone else. In other words, they 'lose touch' with reality. This might involve seeing or hearing things (hallucinations) and believing things that are not true (delusions), possibly leading to anti-social delusions such as paranoia.

(Continued)

Depressive episodes	(Although depression as a singular mental health condition has been covered previously, there are nonetheless some features that are commonly associated with bipolar).

- Feeling severely worthless, as though one's life has little or no value.
- Suicidal ideation.
- Feeling sad or indifferent, leading to decreased activity levels in most areas of life.
- Pessimistic, in despair.
- Fatigue or lacking energy and motivation.
- Lacking self-confidence, persistent self-doubt.

Behavioural symptoms

- Significant and noticeable reduction in activity/productivity. While in some cases people with depression can function sufficiently to engage socially, professionally or educationally, the extreme feelings of depression associated with bipolar can be heightened to the point of rendering an individual almost unable to continue with any endeavour.
- Difficulty sleeping or sleeping too much.
- Low energy levels and long-term fatigue can hinder concentration, affect decision making and lead to hesitancy in many life events.
- Weight loss or gain may be noticeable as the individual's eating patterns may become disrupted. Loss of appetite, comfort or binge eating are all behavioural characteristics of bipolar. As well as poor nutritional intake, a depressive episode may also lead to excessive drinking or substance misuse. Any one or combination of these will over time have a significant impact upon the health of the person.

There are several options for bipolar disorder. Although prescription medication may be part of that treatment, it is unlikely that medical intervention alone will constitute the entirety of the treatment. While universities have a responsibility to 'support' students with bipolar, again it must be acknowledged that the sort of support available (academic adjustments) is probably only a fraction of the whole.

Many people with bipolar disorder will be treated using a combination of medical and psychological treatments, so if the circumstances allow and it is appropriate, asking the student about the nature of their previous or current support is advisable.

The environment and adjustments

It is *the* distinguishing feature of the social model of disability that the relationship between an individual's conditions and their environment is complex. Bearing this in mind, it is the university's responsibility as a whole to understand how environmental pressures may contribute to the presentation of symptoms. As mentioned previously, higher education institutions can be environments with the potential to trigger the onset of mental health deterioration or exacerbate pre-existing conditions. Studies have suggested that biological or genetic factors may be attributive conveyers of mood or behavioural dysregulation, but ultimately, environmental precipitants play a much more important role in the model of, for example, bipolar's presentation. Youngstrom and Perez Algorta (2014: 155) suggest that environmental triggers could include 'interpersonal stressors, dietary factors, [or] disruptions of circadian rhythms'.

Moderating environmental factors through mostly academic reasonable adjustments is not something likely to completely mitigate against the duration, frequency or impact of a mental health condition. This is especially the case for bipolar disorder for two reasons: firstly, as well as a seriously high suicide risk, bipolar disorder has the highest prevalence of comorbidity with other mental health conditions such as depression, general anxiety disorder, ADHD, substance misuse and other addictive features. Managing a condition that presents in such a profuse manner necessitates the scheduled arrangements of timely reviews to determine the effectiveness of adjustments and the extent to which the student is academically progressing. Secondly, the importance of monitoring institutional adjustments in tandem with students' other treatments is something that should be factored into their support plans. Bipolar disorder, severe depression, OCD and other serious mental health illnesses are not conditions that are easily managed without professional help, which necessarily means that regular reviews, feedback and dialogue are formalised with the student and are a primary feature of their university experience.

Adjustments ideally should not be a one-time-only event. Subsequent adjustments thereafter can be amended depending on how well or otherwise the student's mental health is affected by their university experiences. Support plans are flexible documents and must accurately reflect the mental health of the student as much as possible in real time.

Mental health anticipatory adjustments

Establishing boundaries: pastoral care and support

Supporting students in higher education can take many forms, of which academic and pedagogic adjustments are only a part. A welcoming learning environment means taking time to develop good positive relationships with students, one built on mutual trust and understanding, so being sympathetic and empathetic are to be encouraged. In many ways, strong relationships founded on these elements can contribute in not insignificant ways to

Activity	MH impact	Environmental impact	Adjustments
Lectures/ seminars	- Lack of motivation. - Low energy levels, lethargic. - Unfocused, loss of concentration. - Panic attack leading to one or multiple physical sensations, for example, shortness of breath and trembling. - Anticipatory anxiety of content, for example, course content (this is of particular concern for students with PTSD whose symptoms may be triggered by associative subject content). - Fluctuating attendance/ regular missed sessions. - Unprepared for teaching sessions, for example, not reading course material and forgetting items. - Excitable (OCD/bipolar), possibly disruptive.	- Large groups can feel intimidating. - The physical space may induce feelings of claustrophobia. - If the student is unsure of the structure of the session, they may panic or become distracted by anxiety. - Requiring students to speak publicly can feel overwhelming. - Presenting unstructured or unclear material can be difficult for students to follow if their concentration is reduced.	- Clearly structure all sessions; provide an outline of the content. - If discussion or any form of public speaking is planned, work with the student. They can be reassured that engagement is not compulsory, for example. Alternatively, allowing students time to prepare emotionally and psychologically can help – provide materials in advance to aid in their preparation. If possible, liaise with HEI wellbeing/MH team to develop strategies on confidence building – but only if the student fully agrees with this. - Provide warnings if you feel the content may be upsetting or difficult to handle. This should be reiterated as the course outline ought to include this information. - Reassure all students that if they wish to leave the session at any time for any reason they can do. - If possible, allow space near the exit for students likely to experience panic attacks to sit. - Monitor attendance; try to identify as soon as possible those students whose engagement is sporadic or reduced – check to see if they have a support plan; liaise with student support service on engaging the student; allow opportunities for the student to request catch up sessions.

Mental health 53

Activity	MH impact	Environmental impact	Adjustments
Group work	• Social anxiety when speaking in groups. • Inhibited ability to communicate and cooperate. • (For bipolar) sullen/withdrawn or alternatively manic and domineering. • Panic attack (with associated physical symptoms). • Avoiding sessions/late. • Indecisive with fellow group members.	• Group work can be problematic – the anticipation of speaking to strangers can provoke avoidance or missed sessions. • Uncertainty over the roles of each member can cause anxiety/panic. • Personality differences may be difficult to manage due to the onset of bipolar symptoms, side effects of medication or general feeling of irritation.	• Be clear as to the level of participation expected. • Assign roles to groups; each member having their own responsibility towards the completion of the task or undertaking of the endeavour. If communication is felt to be a problem, then ensure that the rest of the group understands that the student does not speak publicly. If the group is expected to work over a longer period, then remote contribution should be considered. • Monitor each member of the group to ensure that all students are provided with equal opportunities to participate. • If necessary, provide an alternative room for the group to work together – this is especially relevant for students overwhelmed by large numbers of people (see also SpLD).

(*Continued*)

54 Mental health

Activity	MH impact	Environmental impact	Adjustments
Presentations	• Extreme anxiety – leading potentially to physical symptoms. • Avoidance – unable to physically present themselves in the class to deliver presentation. • Student may dry up, become mute. • For group sessions, student may be unable to co-deliver fully. • Because of procrastination, the student may be underprepared.	• Size of the room may be intimidating (especially if in a lecture theatre).	• Provide the option for students to request an alternative venue. • If possible, the presentation can be delivered to fewer people. • Instead of live delivery, consider a pre-recorded alternative. • For group presentations, consider individual roles; work with all students to assign roles. If the student is unable to deliver, then ensure that their contribution to the research/creation of the presentation is acknowledged and appropriately assessed. • Allow time for student to pause and collect thoughts. • Allow opportunities for breaks to remove from the situation.
Exams	• Excessive stress and anxiety cause prolonged physical/mental exhaustion. • Panic attack/mind goes blank. • Misses the exam or is late.		• Additional time (25–50%). • Room on own or smaller room with fewer students. • Choice of seating (near the exit, at the back, near the front – depending on preference). • Rest breaks – not including extra time. • Pre-exam preparation – go through previous exam papers. • Assure student that if mental health directly causes problems during the exam, then the student can have the opportunity to retake without penalties (this recommendation is a policy that needs to be agreed by the university).

Activity	MH impact	Environmental impact	Adjustments
Personal organisation	• Students may become overwhelmed, which can result in increased anxiety and stress. • May need to take very frequent breaks to help manage pain and energy levels. • Students experiencing symptom flare ups will not be able to work easily until they feel better. This could have an impact on their ability to meet deadlines.	• Assignment/module deadlines clustered together. • Information on assessment procedures may be difficult to locate. • Too little personal guidance on end of module goal orientation. • Not enough awareness of fluctuating nature of some mental health conditions. • Too little flexibility with attendance and punctuality.	• Opportunity to request and be provided with additional academic guidance from module tutors. • Help breaking down assignment brief – provide clear explanations on what is being taught and how it relates to assignments. • Regular meetings to continue progress.

fostering an environment that may mitigate some of the symptoms of mental health. We know, for example, that environmental triggers can exacerbate or prompt the onset of depression, anxiety or panic attacks, and as Reese and Walker (1997) suggest, 'The student who feels threatened in the learning situation is unlikely to learn effectively'. The emphasis here is 'threatened'. This is not to suggest that university or HE environments are threatening places for students with or without mental health problems or disabilities, but that if students perceive a threat to be real, then their minds and bodies will respond in ways that instinctively are meant to keep them safe (Kennerley, 2014). This can involve behavioural responses such as poor attendance, avoidance and procrastination, to more aggressive and confrontational behaviours. Not all students would exhibit their mental distress in quite the same way, but nonetheless the environment is likely to be a precipitatory factor in the occurrence of their problems. To put it simply, a negative environment will cause negative behaviours.

Logically, therefore, a positive environment will cause positive behaviours. Well, not necessarily. Taking as our example the student with OCD, we know that once the threat level or source of their distraction is fixed, then it takes some considerable specialist intervention to help them regulate their thinking, feelings and behaviour to break their compulsions. It may be that our student is not accessing specialist support and is developing coping strategies to deal with their disturbing thoughts. Conceivably, they may be fixated on some aspect of their university life, whether academic, personal or social. This fixation may involve a belief that some threat is present, one that may be ameliorated through a timely ritual or repetitive invocation of wellbeing. Under such circumstances, a warm and welcoming environment may initially have a positive affect, but we must be aware of the potential for the student's obsessions and compulsions to become conflated with their seeking constant and excessive reassurances. Of course, personal support and general pastoral care are very much part of the staff-student relationship and as such to be expected. For many staff, the nature of their one-to-one meetings is formally established with clearly set out and understood boundaries. But for others, there is often the urge to go that extra mile. There is no right or wrong way to support students pastorally, so formal or informal meetings can work just as well as each other. Developing a trusting relationship with students may develop into a situation in which the member of staff begins to feel that the student is expecting more from them than either academic support or pastoral care. Sometimes, the boundary is clearly discerned, especially if the student explicitly states that they have mental health problems and need **your** support. In which case, it simply becomes a matter of signposting the student to relevant professional services. However, it is not uncommon for staff to feel a certain weight of expectation on them from students who may not necessarily have mentioned mental health or needing support, but who nevertheless make a point of seeking out regular meetings.

The boundary between what is pastoral support and what is specialist treatment can seem blurred to anyone unsure of themselves in such situations, which means there may be dangers of providing inappropriate advice.

This places the member of staff in a situation in which they must navigate the subtle nuances of providing support to a student with mental health problems while not specifically providing mental health support. Naturally, this rather begs the question as to how one should go about not being a counsellor.

Firstly, **establish the reason for the meeting**. Communicating to the student the purpose of any meeting immediately sets appropriate boundaries. While this may be straightforward enough if the focus is academic or subject related, it's not so easily done if it is a general pastoral, welfare check. Start the meeting with some of the following phrases or variations upon:

- Thanks for taking the time to come and see me, I just thought you might appreciate a catch up to see how you're getting on with the course.
- I thought now might be a good time to see how you're settling in at the university.
- I thought we could discuss how you think you're getting on, but please feel free to ask me anything you're unsure about.
- Should the student arrive unannounced, then again, it is important that the reason for the meeting is established quickly and boundaries set.
- Tell me what seems to be the issue. (Try not to commit yourself to offering help at this point, as it may be beyond your professional purview.)

Secondly, **review the purpose of the meetings.** Staff can feel wrong-footed in situations when the student's emotional distress or mental health is such that immediate action is assumed to be required. Our instinct when confronted by anybody in distress is to offer support. Staff therefore need to be aware of the motivating factor for the student's attendance. If the meetings become more frequent and noticeably more regular, then it is advised that time is taken to reflect on their practical utility. Some students simply enjoy the company of their favourite tutors, others may view the help and support they receive from certain members of staff as vital to their wellbeing. Whatever the reason, if scheduled catch up or pastoral meetings reach a point where their frequency is not only noticeable but also focused almost exclusively on feelings or general wellbeing, then it may be that the student has developed an attachment with that member of staff or sees their role as part of their mental health support.

Listening to the student's concerns and asking focused questions will help maintain those all-important professional boundaries. Examples are as follows:

- You seem upset, do you want to tell me what happened?
- I can see you're upset now, but how did you feel earlier?
- Have you spoken to anyone else about this?

- Why do you think you feel this way?
- Do you think someone else in the same situation would feel the way you do?
- Ideally, how would you have done things differently?
- Going forward, what can you take from this?
- If you had to advise someone going through the same thing, what would you say to them?

Thirdly, **stay focused on your own role.** Sometimes, we forget that universities are teaching and learning establishments. If you are unsure about how to respond appropriately, then the following questions can help guide the flow of the conversation, elicit relevant information and help you provide advice and guidance that is appropriate to your role as a professional educator.

How long have you felt this way?

If the conversation focuses upon how the student is feeling or it becomes clear that the student's feelings are causing very real problems, then the first thing to do is ask how long they have felt this way.

The student may answer that they have recently begun to experience feelings symptomatic of GAD or depression, and this has come on relatively recently. Now, ask yourself at what point we are in the academic year; are we approaching assessment periods? It may be approaching colder, darker months, so the student may possibly be experiencing SAD. If it appears that the student has been experiencing negative feelings recently, you may wish to probe further about what is on their mind. They may respond with details about their personal lives or that they have concerns about their workload. But the important thing is that you try to find out whether their experiences have been triggered by events or environmental causes that you can help with. If they reply to say that they have always felt this way or that they often feel down/depressed/stressed/anxious, etc., then this provides us with two important details: firstly, there is likely to be an external trigger to their symptoms, and secondly, the sense of threat they feel to whatever that trigger is, is very likely disproportionate. If the former is something you feel falls within your professional capacity to support (e.g. academic work, time management and feedback), then make a point of focusing on this. However, if it becomes clear, either through the meeting or subsequent meetings, that the student is making demands on your time that appear unreasonable to their academic progress, then a tactful suggestion that they may wish to explore alternative avenues of advice may be appropriate.

Is it affecting your academic work?

This question will help you guide the conversation in a way that can help you offer relevant support. It also focuses the student's attention on how their mental health may be impacting on their work. There are a couple of elements that need to be unpacked here, the first of which is whether the demands of a higher education workload are causing a negative effect upon the student's mental health or whether the student's mental health is having a negative impact upon their academic work. It may be that the two are inextricably linked, but the course of the conversation should allow you to determine if the student would benefit primarily from specialist mental health support with academic advice augmented to that or vice versa. Students' work that is affected because of their mental health is entitled to additional adjustments if necessary. These may include:

- Scheduled study support sessions
- Extensions for coursework
- Alternative assessment (e.g. instead of the student being required to deliver a presentation, provide the option for them to submit a written assessment, a viva or pre-recorded presentation)
- Allow for a fluctuating attendance pattern/missed sessions – with opportunities to catch up

Students with mental health conditions may be taking prescribed medication, the side effects of which may affect energy levels, motivation and the ability to concentrate. Naturally, academic progress could be affected, so modest initial adjustments to the pace of learning and a slight reduction in academic demands may go a long way in enabling a more accessible environment.

Are you currently receiving any specialist support?

This question provides an opportunity to gauge if the student is already in the process of getting help. It also lets you decide whether to suggest that this might be appropriate for the student if they are not. If the student replies that they are receiving support, then the nature of that support can possibly inform your understanding of the impact of their mental health. For example, if the student is receiving specialist support outside of the university's own counselling service, this immediately suggests the likelihood that their mental health is severe and chronic, in which case allowing the conversation to focus on their feelings would not be conducive to good support if they develop an unrealistic expectation of your role.

Have you previously received support for mental health?

This question will help provide context to the student's history of mental health. A student with a history of mental health may have previously received support and have successfully managed their condition until now. If they have previously received support but are not presently accessing any help, then this tells us that their condition is chronic and recurring. This question should also accompany the question as to how long they have felt this way, as it enables the student to give a clearer picture as to what the potential trigger points are, what your role in their overall support is and what adjustments would be appropriate to suit their academic needs.

References

Craske, M. G., Rauch, S. L., Ursano, R., Prenoveau, J., Pine, D. S. and Zinbarg, R. E. (2009). What is an anxiety disorder? *Depression & Anxiety*, 26, pp. 1066–1085.

Harvard Medical School. (2021). https://www.health.harvard.edu/topics/depression

Hawkes, J. (2019). A quick reference guide to mental health on university campus: A brief rhetorical analysis of fear. *Disability & Society*, 34(1), pp. 162–168.

Kennerley, H. (2014). *Overcoming anxiety: A self-help guide using cognitive behavioural techniques*. Robinson.

Mind. (2021). https://www.mind.org.uk/

Müller-Oerlinghausen, B., Berghöfer, A. and Bauer, M. (2002). Bipolar disorder. *The Lancet*. 359(9302), pp. 241–247.

NHS (2021). Panic Disorder. https://www.nhs.uk/mental-health/conditions/panic-disorder/

National Institute for Health and Care Excellence. (2018). How Common Is It? https://cks.nice.org.uk/topics/obsessive-compulsive-disorder/background-information/prevalence/#:~:text=Studies%20have%20estimated%20the%20population,are%20similar%20throughout%20the%20world.

National Institute for Health and Care Excellence. (2022). Depression in adults: Treatment and management. NICE guideline [NG222]. https://www.nice.org.uk/guidance/ng222

National Institute of Mental Health (NIMH). (2022). Transforming the understanding and treatment of mental illnesses. https://www.nimh.nih.gov/

OCD UK. (2021). https://www.ocduk.org/

World Health Organization. (2021). Depression. https://www.who.int/news-room/fact-sheets/detail/depression

Youngstrom, E. A. and Algorta, G. P. (2014). Pediatric bipolar disorder. In E. J. Mash & R. A. Barkley (Eds.), *Child psychopathology* (pp. 264–316). The Guilford Press.

Chapter 3

Visually impaired/blind students

Case study – Karl

Karl is almost totally blind. He was born with limited sight which progressed throughout his childhood until by the time he came to university he had minimal visual acuity. He had informed his university during the application stage of his disability and had contacted his accommodation officer to inform them that he would be bringing onto the campus his guide dog. Throughout the summer, the accommodation officer ensured that Karl would be allocated a ground floor flat near to his main teaching area and that other students who had also booked rooms on the same floor were informed that they would be sharing some space with the guide dog. Karl was also invited onto the campus to help with orientation. Working with his academic department, his classes were timetabled in advance to help him navigate the campus before the start of the academic year. His university's disability services also arranged for a sighted guide to be available during some evenings and weekends, while the library worked closely with his tutors to ensure core reading was available in suitable formats.

The fact that we rely on sight to the extent that we do make it somewhat understandable for so many to assume that any deprivation of this ability is a marker of deficit. But here we must acknowledge the sheer prevalence of blindness and visual impairment, as well as the inequitable experiences of people who are blind or partially sighted. The World Health Organization (WHO)

DOI: 10.4324/9781003223962-4

estimates there are 2.2 billion people globally who are blind or sight impaired, of whom over 1 billion people could have been treated or have had their condition prevented with access to the right resources. WHO states that 'A person's experience of visual impairment varies depending on many factors. This includes, for example, the availability of prevention and treatment interventions, access to vision rehabilitation (including assistive products…) and whether a person experiences problems with inaccessible buildings, transport and information' (WHO, 2021). Clearly then, given the sheer numbers of blind or partially sighted people, the location of their disablement is to be found within a society catering for mostly fully sighted individuals. Arguably, the severity or otherwise of the actual condition is only one factor to the severity of otherwise of their disablement. As WHO clearly states, inaccessible buildings, transport and information are all key features that play their part in the experiences of blind people.

You have probably noticed the use of terms such as blind, visually impaired or sight impaired. Visually impaired people are not totally blind, but the circumstances of their respective conditions do mean that full and active participation in educational activities will probably be restricted without the right support and adjustments. Therefore, before considering what sort of support would most benefit the student, it is worth noting how vision impairment (VI) is categorised.

Vision impairment, according to The International Classification of Diseases 11 (2018), is categorised into mild, moderate, severe and total blindness. Mild, moderate or severe visual impairment may mildly or moderately affect peripheral or central vision, or a student may have problems accessing learning materials because of moderate or severe generalised haze or blurred vision.

This is a key point as blind/visually impaired students do not uniformly lack full sight to the same degree, and even for those where there is a similar level of impairment, there may not necessarily be a comparable set of lived experiences. When putting together support for students who are visually impaired or blind, the following points need to be considered:

- The official diagnosis. This will provide much information on the physical symptoms.
- Whether the student's condition is degenerative. It is not uncommon for people registered as sight impaired to experience decreasing vision as time goes on. If this is the case, it is important to note that the nature of their support and inclusive adjustments must be flexible and regularly reviewed for updates/amendments.

- How long the student has been blind or visually impaired. A student who has been long-term sight impaired is likely to have found strategies to adapt to their environment in ways that someone who has recently become blind or visually impaired has not.
- Physical resources the student either already has or will require. Some blind/VI students may use a cane, others may have a guide dog. Some students may require the assistance of a sighted guide or combination. Whatever their needs, find out as soon as possible what they already have and what you may need to provide.

Students' needs will vary depending on the severity of their impaired vision, when the sight loss occurred and what internal/external support resources are necessary for their inclusion. To that end, we must now consider some of the common types of visual impairment and their effects. Understanding the nature of the condition will enable you to consider the most appropriate adjustments to suit the individual needs of the student. Please note, however, that what follows is not a definitive list of all sight impairments, merely an overview of some of the most common.

Blurred vision

Blurred vision occurs when an individual cannot see the fine details of items they are looking at. Objects would appear hazy or unfocused as the person's eyes cannot pick up light signals sharply.

Blurred vision can occur in both eyes or one eye, with the impairment varying from mild to severe. Possible causes of blurred vision can include conditions such as presbyopia, myopia, hypermetropia or astigmatism but can also be the result of a dislocated lens, a damaged cornea, an eye infection or an object lodged in the eye itself. Blurred or cloudy vision can also be caused by the side effects of certain medications or head/eye trauma. When discussing the support needs of a student with blurred vision, it is worth exploring the possible causes of the impairment as you may need to be aware of the potential for successful treatments, whether the condition is a temporary feature that in time will heal or improve.

Loss of central vision, e.g. macular degeneration

Loss of central vision is often caused because of damage to the macular part of the retina. People with loss of central vision lose their ability to see in detail, making activities like reading, writing, note taking, movement and recognising faces very difficult. Although many diseases can potentially cause loss of central vision, the most common is macular degeneration.

The macula is a tiny part of the retina used to see central, fine detail. As the macula degenerates, it causes blurring and gradual loss of central vision, although the individual's peripheral vision remains intact. Macular degeneration can occur gradually or suddenly, with the condition for the most part being age related, with people over 50 usually affected.

Symptoms of central vision loss can include:

- difficulty reading; printed text can look wavy.
- gradual reduction in vision.
- blank or dark spots in central field of vision.
- distorted or blurred part of the central vision.
- sensitive to bright lights.

Effects on studying

- Difficulty locating reading materials in libraries, online or otherwise independently.
- Reading will be slower, individual word and phrase recognition will be hindered and motivation to continue may reduce over time as the effort to maintain academic progress affects wellbeing and mental health.
- Texts may need to be transcribed which is time consuming, and unless the student is aware of the essential, recommended and background reading, then much time may be lost.
- Light sensitivity may have an adverse impact upon studying in certain areas: e.g. parts of the library, some lecture theatre and classrooms with non-adjustable lighting.
- Loss of central vision will affect students' participation in practical activities especially where there is a requirement to see in fine detail or observe some activities.
- Initial campus orientation will be problematic depending on the severity of the sight loss. Similarly, sudden changes to venues or a requirement to go to an unfamiliar part of the campus may be disabling without the right preparation.
- Note taking from screens or boards will be affected.

Loss of peripheral (side) vision, e.g. glaucoma

Glaucoma is caused by raised pressure of fluid inside the eye. The primary symptom is loss of peripheral vision.

Generally, glaucoma includes blind spots beginning to form in the outer edges of a person's vision. The person may miss things in their peripheral vision, which means in some cases the symptoms may initially go unnoticed. Unless treated, sight loss can progress so that the individual's field of vision eventually reduces to the point where it appears they are seeing the world filtered through a thin tunnel. Central vision may also become affected if left untreated, leading to blind spots appearing in the main field of vision.

Peripheral vision is the part of our field of vision; it occurs outside of central vision and enables most people to see around them without moving their eyes or physically turning their head or body. Peripheral vision helps most people to sense movement and motion in their immediate surroundings, to see things 'out of the corner of their eye'. It is the feature of vision that allows people to undertake seemingly everyday tasks with little effort or concentration.

Symptoms of peripheral vision loss include:

- Poor night vision
- Blind spots
- Light sensitivity – increase or decrease
- Changes in pupil size
- Seeing halos or glare around lights
- Sore eyes
- Headaches and migraines
- Nausea and sickness

Effects on studying

People whose peripheral sight loss is affected often experience seeing the world as though through a haze, which can extend into their central vision. A consequence of this diminished visual acuity is that people with the condition may have difficulty recognising previously familiar words and letters. This will very likely result in the following:

- Taking longer to read texts.
- Longer time reading means preparation for lessons will be difficult.
- Navigating websites, virtual learning environments (VLEs) or portals can be difficult if the design does not allow for sight-impaired people to access them.
- Studying for (multiple) assignments will take longer not just because of slower time but also due to locating appropriate reading resources, note taking difficulties, searching the library and online academic resources.
- Depending on the severity of sight loss, campus navigation may be difficult. Orientation around the campus will be difficult at the point of registration but may continue to be problematic with sudden change to room allocation or venues.
- Handouts and lecture materials may be inaccessible.
- Videos, slides, graphics or illustrated presentations may not be visible or clearly discerned.

- Mid-peripheral vision is needed for reading. When reading line-by-line, we use our field of vision to automatically locate the start of the next line. Also, if we skim read a page or quickly try to find some piece of information, we rely on side vision to aid our efforts. People with glaucoma/reduced peripheral sight experience particular difficulties with these aspects of studying.

As well as reading, writing, note taking from texts or lectures, navigating virtual and actual spaces are all affected by loss of peripheral vision. Eventually, as reading speeds slow further, so tiredness, fatigue and other symptoms such as eyestrain and migraine begin to present. Understandably, then, as reading becomes more burdensome, so comprehension is reduced, resulting in the individual becoming less inclined to read at all.

People with the condition, or who experience the symptoms of glaucoma, may be able to adopt their own strategies to ameliorate the worst affects. These may include:

- Increasing the text/font size when working off a computer screen.
- Using spot lighting to help reading academic material.
- Using a tablet or similar smart device that enables reverse polarity (white letters on a black background).
- Making use of a screen reader.

Adjustments – recruitment and promotional materials

The importance of good promotional material cannot be underestimated. It sends a clear message that the university recognises and anticipates the needs of visually impaired/blind people, so it follows that any institution that values its prospective disabled students will equally value its current disabled students.

By law, all UK universities' websites should be compliant with accessibility legislation which requires public sector websites launched on or after 23 September 2018 to meet accessibility standards. This includes publishing accessibility statements and explaining how accessible their websites are. Compliance with this legislation should not be undertaken simply as a means of ticking all the right boxes, rather the accessible nature of the platform should be given equal importance as any other promotional material.

Websites, intranets, VLEs, institutional apps and e-book platforms must be tested for accessibility by law. There is no need to compromise on the design features of websites, apps etc., but when designing a website, ensure that all diagrams, illustrations, videos and images are annotated, described and transcribed. Your university should have a team or designated member of staff who can advise on designing accessible web content, so when putting together a public-facing webpage, be sure to liaise with the appropriate person to ensure that what you have included can be accessed by students with sight limitations.

Similarly, all prospectuses and all materials available on open days should be made available in accessible formats. It would not be necessary to provide equally the same number of university prospectuses in braille or large print, but it is necessary to ensure that copies are immediately available.

Accessible recruitment practices

During **open days**, it is probably the case that students wishing to attend are required to register beforehand. At this stage, it is advisable that communication is established to allow students the chance to declare their disabilities, and for you to communicate what accessible features are already in place. Remember, students who arrive for open day events also bring with them family members or friends, so bear in mind that even if students' needs are catered for, there is also the potential for discriminatory practices if visitors' needs are not met.

- **Ensure the registration process is accessible**. Make sure there are multiple ways for applicant students to register their interest. These may include emailing the marketing department, registering via an online system such as Eventbrite or via an integrated form on the university website. Online forms can be inaccessible for some blind/VI people who use screen readers or rely on the keyboard to scroll through the website.
- **Promote the recruitment event/open day as accessible**. Reassure visitors that your open day will be inclusive and accessible to blind and disabled people.
- **Promote the open day widely.** Publish as much as possible about the open day; this might include social media platforms, your website and targeted mail shots. Include information on what facilities and amenities students and visitors can expect when they arrive. Provide the following information:
  - Address of the university/higher education institution (HEI).
  - Information on accessible transport routes.
  - Accessible entrances and routes around the campus.
  - Accessible facilities, e.g. accessible toilets, cafes and food stalls.
  - Timetables of any talks or presentations along with detailed information on their location and guidelines on how to access them.
  - Acceptance of guide dogs.
- Make available opportunities for applicants to ask about or request accessible adjustments.
- When costing the event, factor into the budget accessibility requirements. Collecting as much information as you can on accessibility requirements is one way to estimate additional budgetary expenditure. Remember also the

unanticipated costs; undeclared disabilities from students or their family. There is always the potential for utilising some form of non-medical support such as a sighted guide. This can potentially be provided by a designated member staff or volunteer student ambassador or a person/people recruited especially for the event. In either case, providing this sort of support may be fully costed it is always advisable to prepare for unexpected.

- Provide facilities for guide dogs such as bowls for water, exercise areas and, if possible, a spending area.
- Provide audio description during talks or presentations – this is additional narration intended for blind and visually impaired people. These can be difficult to organise but consider whether the use of visuals during a presentation will need audio description.

Orientation and movement – the role of the sighted guide

Orientation is crucial for blind and visually impaired students. It enables them to negotiate safely around the campus and become familiar with their environment. As there is no guarantee that prospective students (or any other visitor) will arrive with any form of non-medical support, it may fall upon the university to provide this kind of assistance as a reasonable adjustment. Understanding some of the basic features of guiding people with sight loss will hopefully create an amenable and accessible environment, as well as give assurance to those providing the support that their help is appropriate to the needs of the individual.

The Royal National Institute for the Blind (2022) has created a very helpful booklet to act as a reference tool for anyone required to undertake the role of sighted guide. The following recommendations are taken from the RNIB's material but adapted for a specifically higher education environment.

1. **The initial approach.** The first thing to consider is that a blind or partially sighted person will probably know how they would prefer to be guided. Unless you are a specialist or work exclusively in the field of sighted guide support, you should remember that you will have considerably less experience of sight loss than the individual for whom your assistance may be required. The sighted guide is primarily there because of their familiarity with the campus layout and knowledge of accessible routes around the campus. Therefore, the person about to be guided should always be asked how they would like to be supported, and crucially, it should be explained what the purpose of the guidance is for. Basically, no grabbing and dragging.
2. **Taking the first steps.** Establish if physical contact is acceptable. Some blind students, unfamiliar with the campus layout, may require in the first few instances someone to help physically negotiate them from place

to place. Others may require a guide to simply walk close to them, either in front or by their side. All cases are individual, and so some students may not need guidance as they become more familiar with the university, whereas others may need assistance throughout the course of their studies. Initially, the student should be asked whether they would prefer for their guide to be close by but not touching, or if physical contact is necessary, whether their preference is for the guide to take their arm or the student to take the guide's.

The RNIB guidance states: *Stand alongside the person you're guiding and hold out your arm slightly for them to take. They will hold your elbow, either cupping their hand against it or taking hold of it lightly. You put your arm where it is comfortable as long as your upper arm is straight. The person you're guiding will walk about half a pace behind you; this makes it easier for them to tell when you're turning your body.*

3 **Know your destination.** With the right preparation, the guide should know where exactly they are going with their student. Some routes across the campus may be more accessible than others for blind people, but never assume that is their preferred direction. Getting from A to B may be the goal, but nonetheless, allowances should be made for the possibility of distractions. These can be walking close to toilet facilities or near to shops and social spaces. If an open day, orientation event or fresher's fair has flexible participation, then this must also apply to blind students. They may change their mind about going somewhere, so it is always advisable to explain route options and what might be encountered en route to their initial destination.

4 **En route.** If necessary, the guide should provide a brief commentary on any barriers or impediments along the route. If this is taking place during an open day or orientation event, then temporary stalls and information points may be present when otherwise they would not be. In which case, it should be explained what is there but continue to state that these will be removed eventually.

A sighted guide should also tell the blind person of any kerbs as they approach. It should be stated if it is "kerb up" or "kerb down". Once the guide has stopped at the kerb, the student will be able to feel the change in movement and come to halt. If possible, the guide should locate the safest place to cross; this could be at a pedestrian crossing or the narrowest part of the road, but either way, the student should be informed about why they have stopped at this part of the road.

5 **Uneven surfaces.** The campus may be located on an uneven surface. This is something that will need to be communicated to the student as soon as possible. If the guide has complete familiarity with the university, then any uneven surfaces, such as slopes or steep gradients, must be explained before setting off. If the guide is not so familiar with the topography of the campus, then warning the student of any inclines of downward slopes is strongly advisable.

Guide dogs

Firstly, guide dogs must be accepted. If an institution prohibits the acceptance or inclusion of a guide dog, then this is direct discrimination under the Equality Act 2010. Universities, therefore, need to accept that an assistance dog as used by a disabled person (as defined by the Equality Act 2010) will require access to the university campus, premises, accommodation and teaching environments. Furthermore, the Equality Act 2010 legally requires institutions such as higher education providers to make reasonable adjustments not just for blind/disabled individuals but also for their guide dogs.

University responsibilities

Universities/HEIs should take responsibility for and provide:

- **Spending pens/area.** These provide the toilet needs of assistance dogs. The location, size and design of the spending area will depend upon several factors ranging from the size of the campus, whether the student and dog will be living on the campus and if the proposed location potentially poses a health risk to others. If the campus does not already have a designated area, then liaison with estates and facilities, accommodation and the health and safety officer should be arranged. There may be some disagreement as to whose departmental budget will cover the cost of the spending area, which means that either agreement needs to be established as soon as possible or the university should already have this set out in its policies and procedures.

    Some universities may simply designate a wide general area of the campus for the dog to do its business on the understanding that the owner takes full responsibility for cleaning up any mess. In such cases, the HEI is at the very least obliged to provide dog waste bins (clearly marked) and take responsibility for the regular emptying and clearing of the bins.

    If the spending area is located inside an enclosed space, then this needs to be made clear to all guide dog owners. It cannot be guaranteed that there will only be one guide dog on the campus at any given time, so consideration must be given to ensure the spending area accommodates the needs of everyone. Certainly, most guide dogs are trained to relieve themselves at specific times of the day or on command, but not all guide dogs prefer going on the same sort of surface. Some prefer hard, concrete or tarmacked surfaces, others incline toward softer, grassier areas.

    If necessary, the university should provide familiarisation and orientation for the owner and the dog. It is worth asking the student how long they have owned the dog as some animals may still be undergoing their training, meaning that initial orientation may help their public-facing skills.

- **Water bowls.** As much as possible, water bowls should at the very least be provided for the guide dog. If the owner agrees to this adjustment, then how and where to access the water bowls should be negotiated.
- **Accommodation and interaction.** If the student and their guide dog choose to live in university accommodation, then the Accommodation Office takes responsibility to ensure that other students are informed of the presence of the dog. Fellow students must also be made aware of the relevant guidelines for interacting with guide dogs.
- Guide dogs are not pets. Therefore, guide dogs should not be treated as pets. Despite this, the charity Guide Dogs UK found that three in ten British people (28%) admit they've stopped and distracted a guide dog while it was working (Guide Dogs, 2021).

    > Such behaviour is potentially very dangerous, especially if a guide dog owner is navigating a busy or unfamiliar environment. If a guide dog loses concentration when approaching a staircase, for example, it could result in a fall and even an injury for the owner.
    >
    > (Guide Dogs, 2021)

- A guide dog for the blind will usually wear a yellow vest/harness. Never touch, pet, feed or physically distract the dog while it is wearing their identifying harness or vest.
- The dog is a working animal so needs to be allowed to focus completely on assisting their owner.
- Unless given permission by the owner, do not talk to or issue commands to the dog.
- Although some owners may allow petting of the dog under certain conditions, do not be offended if the handler asks you not to.
- If the dog is not wearing its vest or harness, this does not necessarily mean it is 'off duty'. It may be resting, so please do not disturb unless you have been given permission to do so beforehand.
- Do not feed the dog or offer it treats.
- If you're walking with a guide dog and its owner, keep to the dog's right side as to do otherwise may cause distraction. If unsure, ask the owner where you should walk. You may be asked to walk ahead of them on their right side or behind.

Accommodation adjustments

For blind or visually impaired students, accessible living accommodation is paramount to their inclusion. The HEI may need to make appropriate assessments of individual needs and put in place physical adjustments to accommodation areas to help students live independently. Depending on the location of the students' accommodation, some areas that could impact on accessibility may or may not be the direct responsibility of the university; this is especially the case if outside areas do not fall within campus boundaries. The RNIB has provided helpful guidelines for outdoor and indoor improvements to living spaces that have been adapted to apply to student accommodation.

Outdoor adaptations

- Identify and repair potential trip hazards such as broken paving.
- Ensure that foliage does not overgrow; some plants may cause an obstruction to pedestrians and especially for blind or visually impaired people.
- Ensure there is a good amount of lighting around the main entrance/exit of student accommodation. Clearly indicate how doors are to be unlocked (e.g. swab, ID card and key).
- Clearly indicate how doors are to be opened, either via pre-registration orientation or clearly signed in large print on the door. Also, door handles should be fixed that are easy to see and grasp.

Indoor adaptations

- For some partially sighted students, natural light is an important feature of their home. Good lighting can enhance visual acuity and minimise the overall effect of their sight loss. Increasing natural light can be achieved relatively easily; new blinds or curtains can be put up. Potentially bigger windows can also be installed, but this may depend on budget, time and willingness. In which case, it would be more straightforward to simply identify what rooms take in the most natural light throughout the year.
- If new windows prove to be prohibitively expensive and unfeasible, then installing artificially controlled lighting is much more reasonable.
- Trip hazards and obstructions such as loose flooring or broken handrails will need to be identified and mended.
- Continuous handrails on either side of the staircase should be fixed.
- Again, depending on time, budget and resources, it may be worth considering redecorating the accommodation's colour scheme. Students can then see objects more easily and tell the difference between rooms.
- Tactile markers and bump dots on appliances are an effective accessible feature for blind students. There are many varieties of inexpensive, commercially available products that can be used to create tactile marking for all sorts of items such as kitchen objects, remote controls and key pads.
- Bathrooms and kitchen areas should have non-stick flooring.

PEEPS – personal emergency evacuation plan

A personal emergency evacuation plan (PEEP) is an individual escape plan for anyone who may not be able to quickly reach a place of safety unaided in the event of an emergency (Worksafe UK, 2021). An evacuation plan's purpose is to aid anyone who cannot easily exit a building. Not all disabled/blind or partially sighted students will require a PEEP, so be mindful not to assume a total absence of independence in this matter. Always check with the students: firstly, if a PEEP is required, and secondly, what sort of assistance is preferred.

When creating a PEEP, the first consideration is how the student will safely exit the building.

- Provide accessible signage so students and any assistant can locate and follow the escape route. Escape routes should be clearly marked.
- As well as accessible signage, it is recommended handrails and step edge markings on escape stairs be installed.
- Braille fire safety signs or audible signs (if possible) must be installed.
- Ensure you are aware of what fire alarm system is installed.
- Make sure fire instructions are available in various formats.

A PEEP also needs to consider the following:

- If the student requires personal assistance.
- Individual, specific requirements, e.g. training and specialist equipment.
- Awareness of all safe routes and refuge/muster points.
- If the student is residing in a multiple-occupancy building – how many other students are likely to be evacuating for example.
- Lifts and stairs – number of stairs, number of flights.

Once these elements have been included in the initial stages of the PEEP, the next step is to break down sequentially the proposed order of events the moment an emergency is declared. This is something that will be individually suited to the student/s needs, so never assume that a previous PEEP that worked well for one student will work just as well for another.

Accessible routes, accessible rooms

For blind/VI students, there are multiple barriers to inclusion within university, ranging widely from limited awareness of the potential impediments faced by students amongst staff (Firat, 2021) to tangible obstructions such as the inaccessible physical characteristics of the campus. A lack of visual acuity, partial sightedness or total blindness invariably makes finding ways around campus extremely challenging, especially where the environment can be busy and subject to change. Recruitment days, induction fairs or organised events can culminate in a location that may be accessible one day but difficult to navigate the next. The unpredictable nature of some spaces not only causes anxiety but also prevents students getting to and from locations. Even when routes are accessible and students have successfully arrived at their intended location, the room itself may pose additional problems for their inclusion. The requirement, then, is how to make the necessary adjustments while considering these factors.

Route planning and travelling can be complex for everyone. Our brains must process visual-spatial information, decode visual markers of locations and potential hazards as well as recall environmental information to either aid our overall familiarity or adapt as circumstances change. In the initial instances of familiarisation, most sighted people would unconsciously assume that in time, travelling between spaces would not require anything like the same effort of concentration. Broadly, the same can be said of blind and VI individuals, but this is not to downplay the challenges to be experienced from even the most independent sight-limited student.

Independence, however, is context-dependent, and in the case of a university campus *being* independent is highly relative. Campuses can be complicated physical spaces to navigate as they vary in size, student/staff numbers, buildings and rooms. Added complexity can involve poor signage, blocked routes, broken lifts, last minute room changes and a whole host of other variables that can prevent a blind student getting to one place from another. But this is not to also overlook the interaction of the student's condition with the physical space; degenerative sight loss, for example, or a condition whereby visual perception may be seasonally affected, all combine to cause the potential for fluctuating disablement as an ongoing issue.

The initial groundwork for enabling physical inclusion can be done with some broad support. We have already seen that orientation is a vital part of campus familiarisation, and its continued inclusion as a reasonable adjustment is something that must be acknowledged. This will depend on the size of the campus (or indeed if students are required to travel between two or more campus sites), as over the course of their studies it is unlikely they will not be subject to room changes. If extra time is therefore needed for students to become familiar with different parts of the campus throughout the duration of their studies, then it must be anticipated that non-medical help (sighted guides) may be needed at certain times of the year, and if so that their availability corresponds with the student's timetable.

Something that should come as standard is accessible signage around campus. Door signs on offices, toilets, lifts and indeed all areas where written signs are located are legally required to comply with accessibility legislation. Providing accessible signs that are tactile (raised lettering) with accompanying braille is a minimum requirement. As with tactile and touch maps, other adjustments may not be feasible as a strictly reasonable adjustment, but introducing a feature such as audio signs might be worth further investigation. Audio signs deliver spoken messages or a warning sound as people approach. They use both visual and sound information to deliver their messages and have been developed to tackle the issue of sign blindness amongst sight-impaired individuals.

Room adjustments

Blind or visually impaired students will require room adjustments. There may be some requirement to organise a classroom differently from one week to the next, but it is advisable to be consistent and not alter the physical space too frequently. The student will need to be reoriented to the room if there have been significant changes between sessions, so bear this in mind when planning lessons.

- Remove visual clutter. This will help the student acquire spatial awareness more easily. Many campus teaching areas are often free from clutter as they are shared spaces, but nonetheless always make sure to check if desk layout has been altered before your session begins.
- Power sockets. Some students may be using specialist assistive technology. If their devices need to be plugged in, orient the student to the most appropriate socket available. This may mean additional attention if students have been tasked to work in groups or relocate from one part of the room to another.
- Students may require more table space to accommodate their specialist equipment and non-medical help (braille, notetaker and computer).
- Likewise, it may be necessary to make available a swivel chair to enable them to move between pieces of equipment.
- If it looks as though the student may be isolated because of their accompanying equipment and support, work with them to ensure the room is adjusted so as not to physically segregate them from the other students.
- As many visually impaired students will have some functioning vision, arrange seating and classroom design by ensuring their sightline is optimised. Arrange desks to allow the student to see both yourself and other speakers.
- Think lighting. If a student's vision is affected because of light sensitivity, then reduce glare by adjusting room illumination. If the room does not have adjustable lighting, then work with the student to experiment with different lights, and if necessary different rooms at particular times of the year.

Non-medical help – the role of the sighted guide and notetaker

Some students may require the use of a sighted guide or notetaker. Please bear in mind, however, that this is not always the case, so when planning for sight-impaired or blind students, be clear as to who is providing what support and under what circumstances. If students are to be accompanied at all times or occasionally while on the campus, staff need to understand that unless specifically stated otherwise, sighted guides and notetakers are not advocates. What this means is that you should not address them instead of the student, nor should you assume they will discuss support needs with you. This is not to suggest that blind/VI support staff are to be completely ignored, indeed there will be times when simply talking to them is unavoidable, but never mistake their role as being more than utilitarian.

Notetakers support students by providing clear and accurate notes of lectures or classes. As notes are essential for learning and revision, the work of a notetaker is crucial. There is no guarantee that the notetakers will be familiar with the subject, which of course means potential problems regarding accuracy and understanding may occur. Even though many students will discuss with the notetakers how they would like their notes to be presented back to them, or what parts of the session should be recorded, it would nonetheless benefit everyone to consider the following:

- Offer opportunities to discuss the session beforehand with both student and notetaker.
- Before starting the session, give an overview of the content, along with a brief outline of the structure.
- Indicate which texts relate to this session – here, you may wish to explore with the student how they might access these texts. Some may be available in audio, others in braille for example. Some texts may be available in large print while others may need to be made accessible though some assistive software packages.
- Explain to the student and notetaker any new technical words or phrases.
- When delivering the session verbally, indicate when moving onto another aspect or topic.
- If using visual images, provide descriptive alt-text to accompany them.

Understandably, note taking for blind or sight-impaired students is highly specialised. Unlike notetakers for sighted students, some specialist equipment such as an electronic notetaker may be used. This is something that can be used by either student or support worker. Electronic notetakers are portable devices for storing information with the use of braille or typewriter keyboards. The stored information may be accessed through a built-in speech synthesiser, a braille display, or both (American Foundation for the Blind, 2021). Other students may prefer to either record sessions or rely on institutional lecture capture facilities. Either way, when delivering sessions, be conscious of the potential for disablement if there is a reliance on presenting anything visual to the students that cannot be accessed through description or an alternative format.

Teaching adjustments – accessible resources and alternative assessments

Blind and visually impaired students' experience of learning is distinct from non-visually impaired students. From getting to a campus, getting around a campus, getting to lectures to getting assessed, the whole experience of studying can be challenging if appropriate adjustments are not in place. Remember, the university is a space that is created to accommodate non-blind people. We live in a visual world, and the world as we experience it has not appeared through a random set of circumstances but has been designed with purpose. That purpose being the inclusion of people who can clearly see the landscape and everything in it.

As a strategy for tackling ableism, it is important to be reassured that inclusion is variable, one that can have multiple meanings depending on the nature of the individual's exclusion, so an adjustment in this respect is not something that is necessarily specialist. A reasonable adjustment is just that – a non-specialist accommodation to ease the difficulties somewhat of blind or visually impaired students. Being cognisant of the main educational barriers faced by students is a step in the right direction towards full inclusivity.

Consider then the educational impediments most likely to affect blind students, and the sort of adjustments that may reduce or address the problem at hand:

Reading

- Blind or sight-impaired students may need longer to read printed material than other students.
- They may require special computer software or equipment (e.g. JAWS, a screen reader and Braille).
- Many blind or visually impaired students read quite effectively from electronically formatted documents.
- It is unlikely blind or visually impaired students can skim read either at the same rate as non-disabled students or at all.
- Reading intensely can cause fatigue or eye strain, meaning that reading can take much longer.
- Navigating a library and finding books will probably require assistance.

The problems here are manifold:

- **Reading materials can be inaccessible**. This can mean books/texts are not available electronically; there is no or limited capacity to adapt reading materials to suit the needs of the students; the physical space of the library can render some texts unavailable; the virtual space of the VLE can similarly prove to be difficult to access without assistance.
- **The physical act of reading can be difficult**. For students with peripheral sight loss, or those whose sight is limited in other ways, physically reading a text may be possible but fraught with complications. Think about it this way; the physical discomfort that can come with struggling to read at length is to assume that blind/VI students should never have the option to skim read. It takes the position that sight-impaired students are necessarily more studious than their sighted counterparts *because* they are blind or visually impaired. The fact that students are known to engage in deep or surface reading is well documented, but not so well known are the reading strategies of blind/VI students. Are we to say that surface learning (skim reading or so-called 'quote hunting') should be the exclusive preserve of the sighted? Of course not. But equality of access is also about providing equal opportunities to study as deeply or superficially as anyone else.
- **Not all books/texts are available**. This is about reading lists. You need to ask how students can access the texts you recommend or make available, as some totally blind students may need completely alternative formats, such as braille or audio. Others may require more personalised adaptations such as large print or select passages of text put through a screen reading package.

Suggestions for adjustments

- Identify core reading before the semester; if possible, identify which texts fall into the categories of essential, recommended or background. Communicate this to students as early as possible and advise which texts are available in what format. Ideally, all texts should be equally accessible, but if this is not possible, you have a responsibility to know whether textbooks are accessible in braille, audio or large print.
- Blind or visually impaired students may need to reformat or obtain alternative versions or transcripts of the texts, so if possible, it would be helpful if key chapters are identified.
- Work with students as they develop their reading skills. This may mean setting aside extra one-to-one sessions for additional guidance, but it would be very helpful if academic staff and support staff worked closely with blind/VI students as they develop their own academic skills.
- Even if some students have carefully developed their study skills, we can still accept that reading is an activity that will probably take longer for

sight-impaired students. Extra time to prepare, to complete assignments and for exams is very strongly recommended.

Written work

Because of the additional time required to read, locate and possibly reformat texts, there may be significant delays in starting the writing process for any assignment.

- Feedback; ask the student for their preferred method of feedback; e.g. verbal (in person), emailed, submitted on their assignment.
- As proofreading may be problematic, let the student know in advance how flexible you can be with spelling, grammar, formatting and citation inaccuracies.
- Extra time is certainly recommended, so if the student has not yet developed their study skills, then more time may be necessary in their first year than their second or third. For this reason, the recommendation for regular additional sessions is repeated – staff need to know at what rate the student is progressing and at what rate they are improving over time.

Group work

Initially, blind or visually impaired students may have concerns about how other students could react to their disabilities. Agree ground rules and expectations, assign group members and roles where necessary and monitor progress. Agree with the student in advance how they would prefer to be included into small group work activities. Take your cue from their advice and guidance.

References

American Foundation for the Blind. (2021). https://www.afb.org/Firat, T. (2021). Experiences of students with visual impairments in higher education: Barriers and facilitators. *British Journal of Special Education*, 48(3), pp. 301–322.
Guide Dogs UK. (2021). https://www.guidedogs.org.uk/
Royal National Institute for the Blind (RNIB). (2022). How to Guide People with Sight Loss. https://media.rnib.org.uk/documents/How_to_guide_people_with_sight_loss_2022.pdf
Work Force UK. (2021). https://workforce.uk.com/
World Health Organisation. (2021). Blindness and Vision Impairment. https://www.who.int/news-room/fact-sheets/detail/blindness-and-visual-impairment

Chapter 4

D/deaf hearing impaired

> **Case study – Saddiq**
>
> Saddiq has partial hearing loss in one ear and is totally deaf in the other. He had chosen to study computer science, which although it required him to spend long periods in front of his computer screen, nonetheless also required him to sit through several hours of lectures and seminars. Although Saddiq used hearing aids, one problem that arose soon after he started his course was that they could not easily filter the ambient noises of a large lecture theatre. Low-level talking, the hum of the room's air conditioning and other electronic devices as well as some sounds emanating from outside, all came together to obscure much of what was being said. It was arranged for some adjustments to be made. Firstly, all lecture and teaching materials were forwarded to Saddiq 24 hours in advance, and space was allocated at the front of the teaching rooms for him. Before each session, the tutors were advised to close windows and/or turn off any unnecessary electrical devices. If the tutors used any video clips during their lectures/seminars, they were advised to ensure captions were available and if necessary full transcripts be made available.

Today, 430 million people (or 5% of the global population) 'require rehabilitation to address their "disabling" hearing loss' (World Health Organization, 2021), of whom 34 million deaf children often receive inadequate schooling. Whether in developing countries or wealthy industrialised nations, education for deaf people remains consistently low. In the UK, the National Deaf Children's Society (2021)(NDCS) states that 'On average, deaf children have achieved an entire grade less than their hearing classmates at GCSE for *at least* the last five years' (as from 2019). They continue to state unequivocally that, 'deafness isn't a learning disability and the results show that education policy is failing deaf children'.

This point is crucial to our understanding of deafness, as well as the extrinsic and intrinsic causes of disability. The notion that deaf students are more likely to fail, drop out or achieve lower marks than their hearing counterparts is sadly confirmed by the NDCS's analysis of government data which found that deaf pupils in England struggle 'at every stage of their education'. Extrinsic (social) causes of deaf/hearing-impaired higher education disablement, therefore, can include a number of factors ranging from environmental designs that privilege the hearing (formal and informal spaces, classrooms, lecture halls, oral and aural communication), segregating deaf students away from their hearing peers to malfunctioning accessible technology, a lack of accessible resources and little leniency in deadline submission dates or alternative assessments.

Before we explore the adjustments, we shall briefly examine the different categories of deafness, not to reduce the experience of *being* deaf to a medicalised pathology but to highlight that with so many other disabilities, deafness is a condition that presents in many ways.

Hearing impairments and their effects

Sensorineural hearing loss

Sensorineural hearing loss is one of the most common types of hearing impairments. It occurs from damage caused to the inner ear, particularly the tiny hairs in the cell walls of an individual's ear. The damaged hair cells prevent sound energy from reaching the cochlea, thus reducing an affected individual's ability to hear clearly across a range of frequencies. More broadly, sensorineural hearing loss 'refers to any cause of hearing loss due to a pathology of the cochlea, auditory nerve or central nervous system' (Tanna et al., 2022).

The causes of sensorineural hearing loss can vary. Therefore, it is important that when discussing possible adjustments with students to discuss how long they have experienced their hearing loss and, if known, the probable cause. Understanding how and why a student has been hearing impaired will give some idea about any coping strategies they might have developed, and whether the condition is likely to deteriorate or improve. In the case of sensorineural hearing loss, causes can include being subjected to excessive sound, especially one-time loud noises such as an explosion or industrial noise.

Acquired hearing loss can also include the onset of age as well as previous exposure to prolonged noise such as a working environment that was/is louder than 85 decibels. Exposure to infections, measles, mumps and meningitis, for example, are also causes of sensorineural hearing loss, as are medical conditions, most noticeably tumours located in the inner ear. There is also every chance that while assessing a student for one condition, it becomes apparent they actually have two or more. This may be the case for students who have been prescribed certain medications as treatments for seemingly unrelated conditions, the side effects of which cause permanent hearing loss. Some cancer treatment drugs, antibiotics and anti-inflammatory medications have been known to cause mild, moderate or severe deafness.

If hearing loss is not immediately noticed, then certain changes in behaviour could indicate a gradual decline in loss. These may include straining to hear lectures; sitting closer to the front of lecture halls or classrooms; not following the thread of discussions, or missing parts of words and phrases during one-to-one conversations or group chats. Welfare issues may additionally present themselves if hearing loss, especially sudden or deteriorating hearing loss, causes students to become increasingly withdrawn and isolated. As acquired hearing loss mostly occurs gradually, symptoms as they relate to higher education may fluctuate depending on several factors such as room acoustics, use of audio-media or even tone of voice from tutors.

Generally, people with sensorineural hearing loss will experience a diminution of a range of sounds within certain contexts:

- Difficulty hearing background noises
- Problems following speech because of background noises
- Missing the thread of conversations if two or more people are talking
- High-pitched aspects of speech may be missed (e.g. 'sh' 'ch' 'th' sounds – this phonetic problem similarly relates to problems experienced by students with dyslexia who also have problems discerning the subtle nuances of spoken language)
- Struggles to hear in noisy areas ('noisy areas' of course being a relative term to each individual)
- Certain sounds may seem excessively or disproportionally loud in one ear
- Tinnitus/ringing in the ear

Treatments vary for sensorineural hearing loss, with hearing aids being the most common. But while hearing aids may help manage an individual's impairment, for the most part, hearing loss will be permanent.

Conductive hearing loss

Like sensorineural hearing loss, conductive hearing loss can be categorised as mild, moderate or severe. Unlike sensorineural hearing loss, there is a greater chance of temporary impairment depending on cause and treatment. Conductive hearing loss is when the individual's ability to hear at a normal level is reduced for some reason. It occurs when the ear's ability to conduct sounds to the inner ear is compromised, resulting in the person affected not being able to fully pick up the full field of noises around them. Causes can vary from physical trauma such as head injury, to blockage by a foreign object. Possible causes of conductive hearing loss also depend on which part of the ear (outer or middle) has been affected. For the outer ear, potential causes can be a build-up of ear wax; otitis externa (swimmer's ear); and exostosis (surfer's ear) or a narrowing of the ear canal. This form of hearing loss can occur gradually, so while assessing the needs of the student, it is advised that a holistic interest is taken that encompasses both symptoms and lifestyle. There may be attributable lifestyle causes that explain both the reason for the impairment and by extension the adjustments required. For example, with swimmer's ear (otitis externa) hearing loss, although compromised, will probably not be permanent. But in the case of surfer's ear, the two bony swellings (exostoses) that gradually appear on the lower wall of the deep part of the ear canal can get worse if certain activities continue.

Conductive hearing loss linked to the middle ear may include an excess of fluid, inner-ear infection, inflammation or a collapse of the ear drum. In such cases, medical treatment is urgently recommended.

Generally, symptoms of conductive hearing loss can include:

- Muffled hearing (problems hearing with clarity, e.g. constantly needs to turn the volume up on television or media technology)
- Full or partial hearing loss
- Dizziness or loss of balance
- Tenderness or pain in the ear
- Fluidic build-up in the ear
- The sense that their own voice seems different or louder
- A preference to hear better out of one ear than the other
- Feeling pain or pressure in one or both ears
- Frustration and difficulty during phone calls or while engaged in person-to-person conversations

Most cases are not permanent and can be treated, with possible options including regular observations and testing; the use of hearing aids or surgery to correct hearing loss or to implant a hearing device such as a bone-anchored implantable device. Alternatively, for infections or wax impaction, a course of antibiotics may be an appropriate course of action.

Mixed hearing loss

Mixed hearing loss is a combination of conductive and sensorineural hearing loss. This means an individual may have damage to their outer, middle or inner ear, the causes of which can include any of the previous possibilities. As with sensorineural and conductive hearing loss, treatments can similarly consist of medication, surgery and hearing aids of surgical implants.

For individuals with mild or moderate hearing loss, hearing aids may be appropriate, while for people with more severe, profound hearing loss, hearing implants may be the better option.

Neural hearing loss

Neural hearing loss is when there is damage to the auditory nerve. As the nerve is physically unable to pass information, implants or hearing aids cannot help.

Mild, moderate and severe

Mild hearing loss is when a person can hear some aspects of speech but may struggle to pick some soft sounds. Whispers or softly spoken speech can be hard to hear, as can particular phonemes of some words and phrases. Consonants at the ends of certain words can be inaudible, which for some students would make lectures/seminars difficult to follow or result in inaccurate notes and understanding.

Moderate hearing loss

A person with moderate hearing loss may be able to hear someone talking but experience difficulties understanding what they're saying. They may be able to pick up fragments of words but not the whole word or phrase, thus making the comprehension of entire sentences extremely difficult. The educational impact of moderate hearing loss will of course vary from person to person, but broadly there will be associated difficulties not just with oral and aural communication but with spelling and reading. Cognitively for some students, there will be a dissonance between the sounds of words and their spelling; in short, if the student cannot hear individual units of sounds in words, these phonetic deficits may affect their spelling.

Mild and moderate hearing loss will also make contributions to class discussion or group work difficult without the right adjustments. Some students may have developed their own coping strategies such as finding the most acoustically appropriate place in the room, or simply asking people to repeat what they have just said. However, despite these techniques, other potentially disabling aspects may be completely out of their control, with ambient background noise, constant chatter or faulty hearing aids being obvious examples.

Severe hearing loss

If a person has severe loss, they will find it extremely difficult to hear another person speak at a normal level and, in most cases, will only be able to hear very loud noises. How an individual experiences their hearing loss will depend on several factors; they may have lost their hearing suddenly due to illness, infection or accident, for example. Or the individual may have gradually lost their hearing, with the expectation that there will be a continuous decrease over time. Some deaf or hearing-impaired students may require the assistance of a specialist notetaker or sign language interpreter, while others may have developed a preference for lip reading.

Adjustments

Teaching spaces and acoustics; seating arrangements and where to stand

To ensure the student has the appropriate adjustments, there are several stages in the assessment process that should be followed. Remember, you are endeavouring to determine the potential environmental causes of their disablement. This means exploring with the student the intersection between their impairment, their experiences of it and the wider institution.

1 Determine the severity of the hearing loss. Ask if the student is mildly, moderately or severely hearing impaired. This will provide you with information about potential barriers that may be present in some teaching environments, especially large lecture theatres, classrooms and workshops. It will also alert you to further additional concerns around class discussions, group work, audio-media/lecture capture technology and online teaching sessions. Some hearing-impaired students may communicate well one-to-one, but if their directional hearing is affected, then group situations can be challenging.
2 Find out how long has the student been hearing impaired. Students who have been D/deaf or hearing impaired throughout most of their lives will have experienced their impairment very differently from a student whose disability is more recent. Even if a student discloses they are severely or profoundly deaf, it should not automatically be assumed they would be proficient sign language users or fully accustomed to a world with no sound. If their hearing loss was diagnosed when they were young, then possibly they have already missed aspects of their early years language and literacy development.
3 Assess the student's capabilities. Do not default to a position of assuming that D/deaf or hearing-impaired students have no hearing capabilities whatsoever. In other words, avoid the deficit model. For many hearing-impaired students, there will be some capabilities that will allow you to make an informed recommendation for adjustments. For example, reserving seats near or in front of lecturers, recommending teaching staff remain in one place during teaching sessions or arranging for microphones to be used during lectures/seminars.

4   Find out if the student uses a hearing aid/cochlea implant: A cochlear implant is an electronic device that provides sounds to a D/deaf individual. The device is in two parts: an external section that is located behind the ear and another section, surgically implanted, under the person's skin. While a cochlea implant amplifies all sounds, it can nonetheless be physically and mentally debilitating trying to identify and filter individual sounds. Implants can help to clarify speech, as well as allow access to a broader range of environmental noises. A consequence of this is that aspects of speech may be missed, newly introduced specialist terms could be misheard or the student may experience loss of focus as concentration efforts induce fatigue.
5   Enquire whether the student requires non-medical help (NMH). If the student has been D/deaf since early childhood, their first language may be British Sign Language (BSL). They may already have secured external funding for a BSL interpreter to accompany them to classes, but this is not guaranteed. Therefore, enquire if a BSL interpreter is needed, whether funding for this has been agreed and if a supplier has been sourced. Other hearing-impaired students may not require the use of a BSL interpreter but may still require the services of a specialist notetaker.
6   Ask if the student relies on lip reading and body language to aid communication. Many D/deaf, hearing-impaired students utilise lip reading, body language and gestures to support their understanding of verbal information. If this is the case, very specific recommendations will need to be made to tutors about amending their delivery during lectures and seminars.

Adjustments to the teaching environment

The following recommendations are by no means exhaustive and do not apply to all D/deaf or hearing-impaired students. Students should always be equal participants in their own support:

- **Locate the student in the most acoustically optimal part of the teaching room.** If the student's ability to hear is affected by background noise, or if they are located some distance from the tutor or person speaking, then ensuring they are within earshot can help overcome any potential barriers.
- **Speak clearly and carefully articulate any unfamiliar words and phrases.** If a student finds it difficult to hear someone who is softly spoken, then there will be occasions when parts of the session will be missed. The same can be said for individuals with strong accents – although here is a note of caution! It is not advisable that anyone with a strong accent be encouraged to soften or change the way they speak. To do so risks an accusation of discrimination against the speaker, especially in a higher

education setting that may be comprised of many international staff and students.
- **Remain as close as possible to the D/deaf, hearing-impaired student.** Students with mild or moderate hearing loss, as well as those who rely on hearing devices, will benefit from speech being delivered at relatively close range. Speaking clearly and being in close physical proximity to the student will also help lip readers.
- **If possible, provide lecture materials in advance.** Many students are reliant on the written word to support their understanding of the subject; therefore, it is beneficial to make available materials ahead of lectures and seminars. This will allow students to read around the subject and help their understanding of new terms, phrases and concepts. Releasing lecture materials in advance will also help hearing-impaired students more readily understand unfamiliar lip patterns and sounds.
- **Sympathetic marking for form and content.** Many D/deaf, hearing-impaired students with language difficulties may not feel they can effectively express themselves in writing. Spelling new words, especially subject-specific terms, may be an aspect of their writing with which they lack confidence. To that end, there may be a reliance on using simple or practiced language that does not represent their actual level of understanding. It is also possible students' work may contain mistakes, misunderstandings or fragmented information. Mishearing information during lectures and seminars is likely to result in errors or misinformation being present in their assignments.

How to work with students who lip read

Lip reading is not an exact means of communication. As much of it requires sustained focus, as well as educated guesswork, there is a high likelihood that meaning may be lost, mistranslated or misunderstood. Even for students who possess some hearing, auditory memory will not be as useful to them as it would be for other students. While most students will pick up on vocabulary assimilation at a relatively swift rate, deaf students may progress significantly slower because of the perceived disconnect between the spoken and written word. For most people, possessing an 'inner voice' while reading is an integral part of the overall reading experience. This is because with language acquisition comes auditory memory (the ability to remember things we hear) which is an integral part of the reading process, especially for languages such as English where there is phonetic and graphemic correspondence. Lacking an 'inner voice' while reading means that understanding written words is experienced differently by people who can imagine how written words sound. As with dyslexic students' phonetic deficits, so with some deaf students – a difficulty in the representation of speech sounds will invariably affect how they understand what is spoken and the association with its corresponding written equivalent. It is vital, therefore, that lip-reading students are given every opportunity to fully understand the content of spoken taught sessions.

- **Structure teaching sessions and signpost topics to students.** If a D/deaf, hearing-impaired student is in the class, then consider the difficulties that may be caused because of poor session planning. It is recommended that the structure of the session is explained to all students beforehand – this may include any planned activities, discussions, interaction or media content. Before the session begins, be very clear what the content will be (what main areas will be covered), in what order and what will be expected of the students. This gives hearing-impaired/deaf students time to prepare and anticipate. If a D/deaf, hearing-impaired student is taking their own notes and relies on lip reading, then being able to follow the structure of the session would be beneficial. As would stopping and pausing to allow students to focus on their note taking – lip reading and taking notes do not go together.
- **Before speaking agree in advance on a signal to indicate that the session has begun.** This can be a nod, wave or some other subtle gesture. It is important that the speaker or tutor is in the student's line of sight before they begin.
- **Ensure the room is adequately lit.** Lipreaders will need to see the face of whoever is talking; standing in front of a window or light will obscure the speaker and render them a silhouette.
- **The student will need to see the speaker's mouth.** Covering the mouth with a hand, face covering, food or drink, etc. will inevitably act as a barrier to effective communication.
- **Be mindful of body language.** Often, almost instinctively, we face several different directions when speaking. Speakers will need to be mindful of this, which means it is advisable not to turn away from the student while talking.
- **There is no need to speak slowly or loudly, but equally the speaker should not mumble, yell or wonder off topic.** If the student has accustomed themselves to the speaker's way of talking, a clear lesson outline has been provided in advance, and any potentially unfamiliar terms have been explained, then speaking at one's normal level and pace should be fine. If unsure, ask the student if pace, pitch and tone are right.
- **Multiple speakers are impossible to lip read.** Ensure that only one person at a time speaks, which therefore requires the tutor control class discussions. There should be a pre-agreed mechanism through which speakers can be identified (e.g. keeping their hand raised long enough to allow the lip-reading student to face them). Also, for any questions that have been asked, the tutor should repeat exactly what has just been said before answering.
- **If possible, make use of some form of assistive technology, particularly speech-to-text software.** This will enable the student to follow

the course of the session and minimise note taking if the session itself is recorded. Please note, however, voice recognition software is not 100% reliable and does not transcribe multiple speakers talking at the same time.
- **Lip readers cannot be expected to lip read at a distance.** Keep at a distance between 1 and 2 metres, especially during one-to-one sessions.

Non-medical help – the role of the sign language interpreter

Some deaf students require the assistance of NMH such as a specialist notetaker or sign language interpreter. If a sign language interpreter is in the classroom or lecture theatre, it is important to understand they are not there to advocate for the student. If a staff member or other student wishes to talk to the student, then this should be done directly and not through the interpreter. Remember, the sign language interpreter is there to translate, not mediate. Although many of the above recommendations will still apply for students with interpreters as they will for students who lip read, there are adjustments that are unique to students who communicate primarily through sign.

- **Face the student directly, they will need to see the face of whoever is speaking.** Agree with the student and the interpreter the best location for them to sit. Usually, the interpreter will sit facing away from the tutor or whoever is speaking. This means the student's focus will mostly be on their interpreter, so if any visual content is introduced, the speaker will need to provide opportunities for the student to see what it is.
- **Ensure the interpreter can hear everything that is said – this includes not just the tutor but also other students or contributors.**
- **It is advisable to introduce yourself to the interpreter and ask them if they would like to hear any new or unfamiliar words and phrases.** Remember, they need to translate quickly, so having a chance to become more familiar with subject-specific words will help them more smoothly communicate to the student.
- **Pause and speak clearly.** Sign language interpreters are usually a few seconds behind the speaker. Ask if the interpreter and the student require a break – sign language interpreting can be intense and quite exhausting.
- **The interpreter will know not to comment on or participate in the session.** Apart from clarifying meaning, they should not communicate with the tutor or whoever is speaking.
- **If the student is using their interpreter bear in mind that even though all comments are being 'voiced' by them, only the student should be addressed directly.** This naturally means avoiding saying 'Let him know…' or 'Tell her this…'

Additional classroom inclusion

Even with the best preparation and adjustments, students may miss vital pieces of information if spoken off the cuff or introduced last minute. If, for example, there is a sudden change of venue for the following session, or additional assignment details are being communicated, then some deaf, hearing-impaired students may miss this. Additional vital information should be written, either on a monitor, whiteboard or emailed to ensure any deaf student is not excluded.

If the speaker is writing on a whiteboard, or typing new information on a computer monitor, they should not speak while writing. After the information is on display, give the student time to take on board what has been written or make notes.

Handouts or written material may be used in some teaching sessions, in which case, it is recommended that extra time is provided for deaf students to read the material in advance. **Audio-visual**: When planning sessions, it is easy to assume that any disabled students can overcome their barriers to learning with last-minute adjustments. This is not always the case, especially if adapted information has not been made available for students with hearing loss. PowerPoint slides, video clips or images on handouts are useful teaching aids that can benefit all students. However, for D/deaf and hearing-impaired students, the use of un-adapted technology can make the learning environment inaccessible. When using slides, the tutor needs to continue adjusting the room lighting especially if speaking while the slide is on display. If the room is too dark (possibly to make the slides more visible), then this runs the risk of obscuring the speaker. Leaving a light on or a window open to illuminate the tutor should help here.

Similarly, consider the overall visibility of the room if using video clips. If the student can see the screen but not their sign language interpreter, then this will cause problems if the clip is not suitably subtitled. Even if the clip is subtitled, accuracy of the subtitling will still need to be checked as many online video-uploading platforms make use of unreliable speech recognition software. As with making lecture materials available in advance, so with video clips, especially for the sign language interpreter. If the video contains unfamiliar words and phrases, it would be helpful if the interpreter was provided with the clip in advance.

If audio material is included in teaching sessions, it is good practice to ensure deaf students are provided with an accurate transcription. Arranging transcriptions can be time consuming, potentially resulting in a delay receiving materials other students have already been able to access. Ideally, deaf students should be provided with all accessible materials equally; yet, oftentimes, this is not possible due to a number of factors, including last-minute lesson planning or sudden changes to staffing.

Preparing for PEEPS – personal emergency evacuation plan

When arranging a personal emergency evacuation plan (PEEP) for a deaf or hearing-impaired student, the following initial information should be provided:

- The alarm systems that are installed to alert them of an emergency evacuation.
- Instructions on how to raise an alarm.

Before creating the PEEP, discuss with the student their likely personal circumstances during an emergency. These may include, for example:

- The likelihood of them being alone at any given time while on campus or in their accommodation.
- Whether the student can hear an alarm and if hearing aids are required.
- If they will need someone to alert them in the event of an emergency, and if this needs to be arranged during evenings and weekends.

The fire alarm system is perhaps the most important aspect to cover when creating a PEEP for deaf or hearing-impaired students. As fire alarm systems that rely on sound will be ineffective for deaf students, alternatives will need to be considered. One such alternative is a system that features warning lights. In addition to the sound of the alarm, this system flashes lights to alert people of a fire or emergency.

If your institution does not have such a system installed, then it is good practice to make early preparation in advance of the student's arrival. Collecting pre-registration information will help with these preparations. Ask if the student intends to live in university accommodation and whether the accommodation has an appropriate alarm system. If the building does not have an alarm system, measures should be taken to rectify this. As this may be a significant operation, things to consider will be budget responsibilities (i.e., which departmental budget will cover the cost), the inclusion of other departments such as Estates and Facilities and sourcing a provider for the alarm. Also, familiarising yourself with any existing emergency policies and practices will also help in the creation of the PEEP as there may already be a system in operation to alert disabled students in the event of a fire.

Unlike students with physical or visual disabilities, most deaf students will not need special equipment as part of their evacuation. If they have already been made aware of the fire emergency procedures, they should be able to understand the situation by observing and following the actions of those around them. If the deaf or hearing-impaired student is lone working, then the PEEP should contain instructions on how to alert them. These may include text alert messages (depending on their location during the day) or a designated member of staff such as security officer or student resident mentor making a point of alerting the deaf student during evenings and throughout the night.

Working in groups

Group working can sometimes take place in the classroom during scheduled teaching sessions, while other times, the requirement to work collaboratively will occur outside students' timetabled lessons. Whatever the circumstances, the potential for exclusion and disablement will be there, especially if no reasonable adjustments have been made or those that have been put in place are inadequate. As mentioned at the start of this chapter, information deprivation because of reduced exposure to incidental learning is a major contributing factor to deaf students' lower educational achievements. This means that if specific learning outcomes are meant to be achieved through some form of group interaction, discussion or collaboration, then it is important that the extent to which incidental learning is assumed to be part of the overall experience is considered.

Tutors are encouraged to plan for adjustments for any group work that has been included during taught sessions. Again, including the student as much as possible during the preparatory stage is highly recommended as it avoids unwanted imposition or inappropriate accommodations:

- **What is the nature of their impairment?** Mild, moderate or severe? This will help with understanding how much may be missed during discussions, if a hearing aid is used and whether background noises or multiple speakers will adversely affect their ability to pick on what has been said.
- **Will the student rely on lip reading?** If so, then seating arrangements and lighting will need to be arranged appropriately.
- **How long have they been deaf/hearing impaired?** In other words, have they fully adjusted to their disability or are still learning to live with their deafness?
- **Will a sign language interpreter be required?**

Agree on what adjustments will best work to their advantage during in-session group activities. Examples, or variations upon, may include:

- **Allowing the student to choose group members as people with whom they feel familiar may be easier to communicate with.** This is especially so if the student's friends have already begun to accustom themselves to the needs of a deaf, hearing-impaired student.
- **Assigning roles to group members if necessary.** If the group is asked to work in a workshop or engage in some practical activity, then consider how roles should be assigned. Providing each student with task objectives with clear outcomes will help with both the overall group dynamic as

well as help the deaf, hearing-impaired student make an equally positive contribution.
- **Ensuring the room is well lit, with good lighting for the student to see the faces of all group members.** It may be best to position the groups in a circle or semi-circle, which may require some prior adjustments to the room. Ensure nobody is silhouetted against the light. In lecture halls, this might not be possible, so tutors are advised to find an alternative location where the students can work.
- **Reducing background noise.** As some hearing aids amplify all sounds, it is possible that excessive background noises will be a major impediment to the student's ability to contribute. Noise reduction can be achieved by simply closing doors and windows, switching off or turning down nearby electric appliances or ensuring the room is scheduled in a location away from noisy areas of campus. If possible, check the room is acoustically appropriate, i.e., can better absorb sound with soft carpeting, tiles ceiling or soft furnishing.
- **Taking guidance from the D/deaf, hearing-impaired student it may be advisable to brief the other students on the adjustments.** This will require explaining what the adjustments are and why they have been put in place. Including as many people as possible in the adjustments also helps share the responsibility for inclusion. If the student is a lipreader or uses a sign language interpreter, then the other students should be made aware of this, along with their own responsibilities on what not to do while working, e.g. moving around, speaking at once, talking directly to the interpreter, talking slowly or loudly. If the deaf, hearing-impaired student uses a radio microphone system or loop system, all other group members will need to speak into the microphone.

References

Kusters, A. (Winter 2010). Deaf Utopias? Reviewing the sociocultural literature on the world's "Martha's Vineyard Situations". *The Journal of Deaf Studies and Deaf Education*, 15(1), pp. 3–16.
National Deaf Children's Society. (2021). https://www.ndcs.org.uk/
Tanna, R.J., Lin, J.W. and De Jesus, O. (2022). *Sensorineural hearing loss.* (21 December 2021). StatPearls [Internet]. StatPearls Publishing.
World Health Organization. (2021). Deafness and Hearing Loss. https://www.who.int/news-room/fact-sheets/detail/deafness-and-hearing-loss

Chapter 5

Physical impairments

Case study – three students

Consider the cases of three students; one with cerebral palsy (CP) and severe migraine; another with only CP; and a third with Charcot-Marie-Tooth disease (CMT). All these students experience some form of physical restriction, with the first student being a wheelchair user; the second student reporting right-sided weakness from having to work left-handed most of the time as well as lower back and thigh pain; and the third experiencing numbness in her feet, arms and hands, and muscle weakness in her lower limbs. Each student will initially be categorised as 'physically impaired', and yet each will require their own adjustments. For the first student, there are obvious accessibility issues that would need to be addressed, the most prominent being how much of the campus can accommodate their wheelchair for the 90% of the time they use it, and how much of the campus they can access for the 10% he does not. Our second student's experience of CP has some similarities as the condition also reduces physical mobility, with her also reporting that persistent pain in her lower back and thighs often causes fatigue and exhaustion. Student number one's wheelchair potentially renders many areas of the campus off limits if there are no ramps or lifts, or if the lifts are incompatible with his chair. Unlike student one, our second student's CP does not require her to use a wheelchair, which means potentially more of the campus is accessible. And while student number three also experiences some physical limitations because of muscle weakness in the feet, ankles, legs and

DOI: 10.4324/9781003223962-6

hands, as well as an awkward way of walking, they are nonetheless relatively more mobile than their two peers.

Added complexity comes with the secondary features of some disabilities that regularly accompany their primary conditions. The first student also has a diagnosis of severe migraines which can last for several hours and take maybe one or two days from which to recover. The combined physical and mental impact of two such conditions will inevitably have an impact on their energy levels, focus, ability to concentrate and academic progress.

Similarly, the second student experiences ongoing challenges with fatigue and exhaustion due to restricted mobility; they often must expend a significant amount of energy to get around leaving the student both physically and mentally drained. The student is only able to walk for about 10–15 minutes after which they need to rest. Given the daily physical toll of simply moving from one location to another, there is often a trade-off between their ability to get around and being able to function; often they are so drained by their exertions that it can take several days to regain enough strength to begin all over again. The cumulative effect of these experiences, in addition to the obvious physical debilitations, is also mental and cognitive – their focus, ability to concentrate and maintain any sort of academic momentum is adversely affected. Both students then have secondary symptoms that go beyond physical accessibility. The demands of negotiating even the most accessible spaces are such that attention span, concentration, comprehension and memory are all impacted in their own way, and which therefore require consideration when putting in place adjustments.

For student three, the condition has a marked effect on their studies that exceed whatever difficulties are faced when accessing the campus environment. Like student two, this student will require rest breaks and time out to be able to continue studying. All students for slightly different reasons experience aches and pains after some time sitting in the same position or moving between locations, and all students become physically and mentally drained long before non-disabled students would. But while students one and two need rest to regain lost energy, student three requires breaks to move around which prevents a build-up of pain and stiffness in his hands and feet. Compounding this, unlike students one and two, is that their condition is progressive. This means the symptoms slowly get worse, making everyday tasks increasingly difficult.

So, the impact of reduced or limited mobility is not uniform. Before the student even arrives on the campus, they are beset by a combination of preconceptions and stereotypes, low expectations and a statistical likelihood of failure. Added to this is the physical space of the campus itself, whether it is accessible by public transport or has adequate disabled parking, if there are ramps in the right places, lifts that are not only reliably functioning but can accommodate wheelchairs of different shapes and sizes, entrances and exits that can be opened and closed unaided and learning materials that can be provided without fuss or inconvenience. Further disabling factors include timetabling, curriculum development and classroom management. Students who struggle to make their way to classes and are left feeling drained and fatigued because of their efforts may have accessed their lectures, but if in their exhaustion they lack the energy to focus then it cannot be said that accessibility has led to inclusion. Likewise, if classroom activities involve practical elements or group work, then we should not be surprised if attendance fluctuates dramatically. Similarly, some physically disabled students may not have the energy through the term to maintain the sort of momentum to carry them through to completion on time. Inflexible deadlines or requiring disabled students to go through lengthy application procedures for coursework extensions may do little for their sense on inclusion.

As with other impairments, medical conditions or learning difficulties, physical disabilities are no less varied. Achieving full access and inclusion as a viable outcome for a physically disabled student may be the objective, but what might work for one student may be inappropriate for another. The physical (medical) causes of a person's impairment can include conditions that range from the hereditary or genetic, such as spina bifida, CP, cystic fibrosis (CF), epilepsy, muscular dystrophy or dwarfism, to acquired conditions such as spinal cord injury, head trauma, serious injury, multiple sclerosis (MS), arthritis or motor neurone disease.

Physical disability can reduce an individual's ability to undertake or complete everyday tasks, with problems walking, sitting, standing or moving some muscles impacting on everyday life. But we must be aware that diversity exists within the disabled community, and even amongst those with the same condition. As physical disability affects mobility, dexterity, stamina and coordination, as well as mental health, focus and energy levels, it follows that no one disabled life experience will exactly match another. For example, one student with arthritis may have symptoms that present as joint pains in the hand and wrist, while another may experience restricted mobility issues because the condition is localised in their hips or legs.

If we were to take a medical model approach to disability, the first things we would determine are the physical characteristics and official diagnoses; this would emphasise the significance of symptoms like scoliosis (CP and spina bifida), or difficulties walking, trouble using certain limbs possibly leading to paralysis, bone and joint deformities, recurrent infections or muscle spasms (as random examples). Certainly, there can be consistent symptoms across the broad range of conditions; for example, bowel/urinary incontinence are symptoms of CP, CF and spina bifida, while muscle and joint pains affect people with muscular dystrophy, arthritis, CP and CMT disease. Similarly, problems with movement and coordination occur amongst those with CP, MS, spina bifida and muscular dystrophy, of which epilepsy is often associated with several of these conditions. But the barriers faced by disabled students do not wholly stem from medical presentations. Although the conditions can and do make demands on one's attention, it is the intersection between condition, symptoms and adjustments that either mitigate or exacerbate any further disablement.

Wheelchairs – the barriers to physical access

Note: although this section primarily covers wheelchair users, the same can be applied equally to disabled and physically impaired students who are not wheelchair users.

Wheelchairs are not signifiers of confinement. Quite the opposite – wheelchairs are a means of enabling freedom of movement and independence. Before we detail the physical barriers to inclusion that wheelchair users often encounter, certain attitudinal and cultural barriers must be addressed. The main one being the notion that users are 'confined' to their wheelchairs. We too often hear phrases such as 'wheelchair bound' to describe wheelchair use, a phrase revealing a belief that wheelchair users' lives are limited or intrinsically restricted. This is, according to The Diversity Style Guide (2021), 'misleading, as wheelchairs can liberate people, allowing them to move about, and they are inaccurate, as people who use wheelchairs are not permanently confined in them, but are transferred [or transfer themselves] to sleep, sit in chairs, drive cars, etc.'.

Speaker and author Jenny Smith reiterated this point more forcefully when writing about both the issue of language referral and her own personal experiences:

> Do I use a wheelchair? Yes.
> Is a wheelchair a necessity to live my life? No doubt.
> Am I confined to a wheelchair? Absolutely not.
> I certainly am not confined to a wheelchair. I am able to live life because of my wheelchair. A wheelchair allows me to go to work, to play sports and volunteer. It gives me the freedom to be with friends, to cook dinner for my niece and nephew and to travel to faraway places.
> A wheelchair is freedom.
>
> (Smith, 2021)

The wheelchair, if it is a symbol of anything, is a symbol of liberation and freedom. Misperceptions about wheelchairs unfortunately abound across most of society, reinforcing assumptions that individuals who need them are restricted in their everyday lives. Assuming the very worst preconceived prejudices about wheelchair users also places the onus on the disabled person to challenge these views and overcome their limitations, rather than everyone else to help create a supportive and inclusive environment. This psychological shifting of responsibility, in effect challenging disabled people to exceed expectations and prove themselves in a non-disabled environment, recuses all but the disabled individual from the responsibilities of support. Cultural, social and personal attitudes about disability are not easily relinquished, but a good starting point is divesting oneself of the notion that if a wheelchair user cannot access a particular space that it is a design fault of the wheelchair rather than the space.

As required by the Equality Act 2010, public bodies and organisations, including higher education institutions, are legally obliged to take reasonable steps to remove physical barriers that disabled people might experience when accessing their services. For wheelchair users, physical barriers can include, but are not limited to:

- steps and kerbs
- stairways
- exterior paving
- parking spaces
- entrances/exits to buildings (including emergency escape routes)
- internal doors
- toilets and washing facilities
- lifts

- floor coverings
- signage furniture
- temporary or movable items such as displays and stalls.

The first focus for reasonable adjustments is physical access. Whatever adjustments are put in place will need to be informed by whatever medical/disability evidence the students choose to provide, as well as in-depth discussions with the students and a thorough understanding of campus layout and course design. Therefore, it is best to begin with gathering some base level information:

1 **What is the nature of the disability?** Knowing what the diagnoses are will provide an initial understanding of the key physical impacts. For example, CP is a group of lifelong conditions that affect movement and coordination to different degrees. Likewise, some conditions such as joint hypermobility may also restrict movement, while others like MS or serious injury may localise physical impairment to one specific area of the body. Researching the nature of the condition will yield up very broad information, but more individual information will be needed.
2 **What are the individual symptoms?** By symptoms we mean the primary features of the student's impairment. Take your cue as much as possible from the student here; let them explain how they have experienced being a wheelchair user, or how their manual dexterity has affected their ability to manipulate objects such as pens, keyboards or other devices. This will be more relevant depending on academic subjects; manual dexterity may be less of a feature for studying English than it would be if they were on an electrical engineering degree. But accessing a wider range of reading material from the library may prove more problematic if there is a greater volume of material to read. If the student has any form of physical impairment, then some part of their course will not be accessible without adjustments.
3 **How accessible is the campus/individual buildings for the student?** You will need a thorough understanding of the campus to make this determination. It is important you know the location of all ramps, lifts, service elevators. Explore whether certain areas of the campus will be independently accessible for the student. Many university campuses contain old buildings that pre-date accessibility legislation, therefore rendering them difficult or impossible for some students to enter. You will need to investigate which buildings have adapted entrances/exits, ramps, lifts and what sort of internal doors, toilets and signage they have. If internal doors are closed, can they be opened unaided by a person in a wheelchair, or someone with reduced manual dexterity? Assume that parts of the campus will be less accessible than others, in which case it is advisable that you are aware of how reliable accessible routes are, and what locations should be avoided.

4   **How will the student usually arrive on campus?** If by public transport, then the student will need to be advised whether the main entrance to the campus is accessible from their drop-off point. Are there main roads to cross between the drop-off point and the main entrance? Or are there enough disabled parking spaces available? Some students may prefer to travel on public transport, while others choose to be driven by specially adapted vehicles, or drive themselves to campus. Whatever their chosen method of transportation the likelihood of their being late or missing sessions is greater than it is for non-disabled students. In which case it should be communicated that no penalties will be incurred if their attendance is affected because of their disability.

5   **Does the student use a wheelchair?** Wheelchairs can be categorised as either manual wheelchairs (propelled by the user's own strength) or powered/electric wheelchairs. Possibly the student will use more than one type of wheelchair depending on the physical environment, purpose of use or their capability on some days. Either way, knowing what sort(s) of wheelchair(s) the student will primarily use on campus will give you an indication of whether they will need accessible routes to accommodate larger, electric assisted chairs, if classes will need to be scheduled on the ground floor or accessible rooms, or if personal assistants will be accompanying them some or all of the time.

6   **Which campus routes are accessible?** University campuses come in all sorts of different shapes and sizes. Some are in one location, others are less contained and spread across multiple buildings and properties. Student accommodation can be equally varied, with accommodation found on the campus itself or some distance away from the students' main teaching area. It would be reasonable to assume, therefore, that not all routes between teaching, living and social spaces will be as easy to navigate as each other. Before the student arrives, you will need to know not only which the most appropriate routes are to facilitate smooth navigation between locations, but also if those routes are better suited for one type of wheelchair over another. You will also need to ask if the student will need rest breaks between spaces, and whether scheduled events and classes can be arranged to be less spread out.

Some courses may be more physically accessible than others, so it is advisable to have at hand as much material as possible on all your institution's programmes, e.g., module handbooks, reading lists, assessment criteria, learning outcomes. Work through the material to identify if the content, delivery and assessment of the programme are potentially problematic.

1   **What is the course?** Arts & Humanities? Social Sciences? Natural Sciences? Technology? Maths? The point is to understand what the student will experience in their teaching and learning environment. Are they likely to be engaged in library-based study more than workshop or practical activities? Are laboratories located in one or several locations, and how

accessible are they for manual or electrical wheelchairs, or students with mobility restrictions? Knowing the subject they wish to study will provide some initial insight into how they will spend the bulk of their study time.

2. **What has been their previous experience of support?** Students will wish to make the transition into higher education as consistent as possible. If they have had extra time for exams and extended deadlines for coursework, make sure the student is aware whether these adjustments can be put in place. Likewise, if some element of remote study or allowances made for lab/workshop assistants to be present was part of their previous support, be sure to communicate before the course begins whether these can also be recommended.

3. **Where will the teaching take place?** Arranging for pre-enrolment orientation visits, providing students with campus maps and providing links to 3D campus tours will help disabled students better understand what disabling features may need to be addressed. If a student has arranged to visit the campus while an applicant, it would be a good idea to include various members of staff. Academic staff can provide information on course content; accommodation officers can discuss any adaptations that may be required to student living areas; timetabling/admin staff can accompany students around the campus as accessible routes and accessible rooms are explored. This way once the student arrives, they are already reasonably familiar with the campus layout, they are timetabled in classrooms/lecture theatres that can be accessed and they have a good understanding of the course requirements.

4. **What learning materials will be needed?** Core reading material may be accessed electronically, or perhaps hard copy versions are available in the library. Either way, the student will need assurances that all materials are available in the format that suits their needs. Library staff may need to be informed if disabled students require assistance retrieving books or journals from shelves. Arrangements will need to be made for assistance to be provided to carry books and other materials. Likewise, if the student is studying on a course that requires technical, practical proficiency then staff would need to consider what aspects of which technology could be disabling. For example, a student with CP, who has limited motor coordination, studying electrical engineering or media production, may not have the capacity to manipulate some devices or pieces of technology. In which case it would become necessary to really work with several key people to ensure adjustments are put in place. Ask the student what assistive technology they already have with them; for example, some wheelchair users use remote control infrared devices such as voice boxes that might be made compatible with existing university technology, or there may be specialist equipment already available through external suppliers. If necessary, bring in academic staff, university technical staff and even the manufacturers of the software and hardware that is mostly used by students on the course. Explore every avenue available to adapt or introduce technology that enables the student to access their course with complete equity.

5 **Will the student need personal assistants?** PAs here can mean anything from local authority provided assistants (for daily assistance or physical therapy) to notetakers in class. If the student does require the services of a PA, then this needs to be factored into the overall support and adjustment strategy. Some classrooms may only contain a finite number of seats, meaning that the role of the PA will need to be agreed with academic staff in advance. Moreover, if the student uses an electric wheelchair and other devices, then seating may need to be arranged to position them close to a power source. PAs can also serve as prompts or facilitators for communication, especially for explaining the meaning of certain non-verbal cues for communication.

6 **Does the student need a therapy room?** Some students will need regular physiotherapy or a place to stretch. It needs to be ascertained as soon as possible whether, firstly, the student does need this, and secondly, if there is a place on campus for the therapy to take place. Ideally there needs to be a designated room containing the following: an ergonomic height adjustable bed; ergonomic mattress; hoist; disabled toilet; waste bins (to be emptied daily), and sink. If all these cannot be contained in the same room, then the student will need to know the locations and best routes to the nearest disabled toilet, wash facilities etc. Academic staff will also need to be alerted that the student may require regular use of the therapy room and may be late, missing or leaving early from some sessions.

Accommodation

If the student intends to live in university accommodation, then contact should be made to explore their accommodation options. Talk to the student about what their living/domestic requirements are, what sort of rooms they will need and of course if any physical adaptations will need to be put in place. Remember, for university-owned accommodation, this means:

- students cannot be refused accommodation because they are disabled
- universities must make reasonable attempts to provide disabled students with somewhere accessible to live
- disabled students' accommodation must be of the same standard as non-disabled students

As a matter of priority, disabled students should be given the option to choose the location and room that best suits their needs. For some students, accessible accommodation can be relatively simple. Examples can include:

- ground floor room
- accommodation block near main campus
- their room or flat located close to the lift

Other students might have additional requirements:

- Full wheelchair access – ramp, automatic doors that are accessible to the student
- Power assisted doors
- Minimum door width of 750mm
- Doors with lowered viewing holes
- En suit
- Alarm cord – many universities use specific alarm cords that allow students to call security, first aid or other assistance through their smart phones
- Sockets and switches – light sockets and power points accessible from a seated position
- Height adjustable desks and surfaces (both for study and in the kitchen for cooking, cleaning)
- Storage cupboards, fridges and freezers accessible from a sitting position
- Height adjustable kitchen work surfaces
- Lower handles on doors, wardrobes and draws
- Wardrobes with lower clothes rail
- Lowered or height adjustable shelving
- Hinged shower seat
- Shower and changing tables
- Hoist (in bathroom and main living space)
- Level entry access to shower or wet room
- Accessible toilet – floor mounted; grab bar; surface mounted toilet tissue dispenser
- Accessible wash basins

If the student's disability is such that additional adaptations is required, then it is important to determine what exactly is needed as soon as possible. Several departments will need to be involved depending on the relative complexity of the adjustments. Disability support and accommodation services must work closely to identify which rooms initially meet the student's needs, but also the university's health and safety officer as well as Estates & Facilities for any risk assessments and structural surveys. Unless all departments know exactly how many of the new features will be funded then early progress will be stalled if there is disagreement about whose budget should pay for the costs of the adaptations.

Care workers

Some students require the services of care workers. These can be both medical and non-medical. For students with specialist care workers, access and participation in a range of university activities can be contingent upon their presence on campus. To that end, understanding the role of care workers will help enable academic, social and domestic inclusion.

Firstly, a 'care worker', or 'carer' or 'care giver' can be anyone. Often, they are employed either directly by students' local authorities or indirectly via an outsourced agency. But equally a care worker can be of the student's own choice such as a relative, partner or friend. If the student has decided to live in university provided accommodation, then their care workers may also live with them. This means there will be financial implications if the carer needs their own room next to or close to the student, which in turn means that rent and accommodation policies must be discussed with the student before any contracts are signed.

Some carers may not live with the students whom they are supporting but will nonetheless need access to their accommodation at certain times of the day. This may be to help the student get dressed and prepared, cook meals or pick them up for classes. Occasionally the care worker might need to enter secure and private living spaces. It would be good practice for accommodation, disability support, security and estates to be aware of any non-university employed carers entering student accommodation, ideally with a process in place to enable the carer to gain access by registering their presence on campus first.

In classes care workers will be a visible presence, especially if student wheelchair users are accompanied by more than one carer. This immediately places a barrier between the student and everyone else, meaning that social interaction, group discussions or team working can be severely curtailed. This is an important point as disabled students can be excluded if other students do not feel confident to see past their disability.

Some care workers for physically disabled students will need to be actively engaged in lessons, particularly if they are required to advocate for the student. For example, students with restricted speech patterns and reduced motor coordination will initially rely on their care/support workers to clarify non-verbal cues to communication. They may also act as more practical based assistants in labs, studios or workshops. It is advised that academic staff discuss with the student the role of their care workers during lecturers and seminars, agree on boundaries and appropriate communication.

PEEPS – personal emergency evacuation plan

Personal emergency evacuation plans (PEEP) are documents used to detail the steps that must be taken to evacuate disabled students if they have difficulty responding to fire alarms or exiting a building unaided.

PEEPS must be individually tailored to each student. They should include the nature of the disability, the relevant main parts of the campus (accommodation, library, lecturer theatres). In the first instances, students will need to be contacted with requests for information about their evacuation requirements.

Consideration should be given to the following:

- Whether the student can exit the building unaided.
- The nature of the student's disability – are they wheelchair users? If so, is the wheelchair user self-propelled or electric?

- If the student will be accompanied by a care/support worker.
- Whether the student uses an aid such as a cane, crutches, walking stick, etc.
- How long they can walk unassisted.

At this point it will be necessary to liaise with other departments and services. The health and safety officer and facilities manager will need to be alerted, especially if your university policy is that they write PEEPs.

All locations will need to be included on the PEEP; these include specific buildings, floors, rooms. Added to this is information about assistance required and who will have responsibility for this. Include names and contact details of the student's appointed assistants, where they are usually located along with direct phone number and email address. Also detail their role in the evacuation procedure.

Timetabling and accessible rooms

When arranging classes, give some thought to timing and location. Physically disabled students' access to higher education can be helped or hindered by something as seemingly straightforward as their timetable. For students who rely on public transport or private hire assisted taxis, getting to and from campus at certain times of the day may be problematic. Other students living on or near campus can experience difficulties if their rooms have been scheduled in inaccessible parts of the university, routes between locations are littered with impediments or lifts are unreliable.

Even if the physical environment is accessible, disablement can still occur. Certain physical disabilities can impact on health and energy levels, or students may require physical therapy at scheduled times. For example, spinal muscular atrophy (SMA), a genetic neuromuscular disorder characterised by loss of motor neurones and progressive muscle wasting, severely restricts movement and can require the use of an electric wheelchair, care workers and a therapy room. Students with this and similar conditions will need physiotherapy during the day, meaning that timetabling lecturers and seminars around their physical requirements should be arranged before registration.

An accessible teaching space is vital for disabled students to participate and engage.

- Students must be able to circulate freely around the room. There needs to be adequate space for turning radius for wheelchair users. The turning radius is the space necessary to execute a 180 degree turn in a wheelchair. As a general rule, the space required for a wheelchair is 78 inches (197 cm) by 60 inches (153 cm) minimum.
- Ensure storage areas, lab/studio/workshop equipment, sinks and power sockets can be reached.

- Entrances and exits can be operated unaided or any potential barrier has been addressed.
- Storage space may be required for aids such as crutches, walking frames as well as wheelchairs as some students may wish to transfer to a regular chair during the session.
- Classroom/lecture theatre layout may require careful arranging. Desks and chairs should not impede the smooth flow of movement, so if certain activities have been planned consider the positioning of desks, chairs, equipment and other class furniture.

How to plan for a field trip

All students should have equal access to any planned fieldtrips, which naturally means ensuring disabled students should not face barriers preventing their inclusion. To facilitate full inclusion all potential disabling factors will need to be anticipated. These may include the time and date of the trip; whether it is for the whole or part of the day; if overnight accommodation is included; the fluctuating energy levels of the student, or if the student will be accompanied by a care worker.

Begin by including the student as a co-creator of their adjustment plan. Focus on how the student has previously accessed travelling on trips or visits. Remember, they are the experts in themselves so take your cue from what the student can tell you through their personal experience. To guide the discussion, consider the following:

- **The date and time of the trip**. This may be relevant if the student's disability is seasonally affected (arthritis), or the weather is likely to cause difficulties. Wheelchair users or students who use crutches and walking aids may find it harder to move around on wet or frozen surfaces.
- **Travelling.** How are students expected to make their way to the location of the fieldtrip? If students require specially adapted vehicles there might be logistical and financial implications. Consider whether the university will need to take partial or full responsibility for booking, hiring and paying for adapted vehicles. If the university plans to take students to the location directly, check whether the vehicle(s) is appropriate. Many universities use their own minibuses, so special adaptations for wheelchair access or seating will need to be checked beforehand.
- **If care workers will accompany the student**. If so, then space will need to be provided on transport (if necessary), as well as possible overnight accommodation. Also, if there is a cost implication then it is not advisable for the student to cover the cost themselves. This may include food and drink and, if relevant, entrance fees. If there is a cost implication for care workers on field trips agree as early as possible how those will be covered.

- **Whether medical issues need to be considered.** This could mean providing an appropriate place for physiotherapy or medicine administration.
- **Details for the location of the fieldtrip.** If the trip is to be in a single location such as gallery or museum, find out details of their accessible features. These would include ramps, lifts, accessible toilets and layout. Work with the student to determine most appropriate routes and where to take rest breaks.
- **What activities will be included?** As fieldtrips are intended to be educational expect educational activities to be included. These may be sight visits, observing demonstrations or engaged in some kind of active and participative activity. Natural science students may be required to observe or measure some natural phenomenon using tools and devices that will need to be checked for accessibility. Also, if the students are expected to be out in the field undertaking physically demanding works (archaeological excavations being one example), then consider the impact this may have on a student who is known to tire easily, has low energy levels and reduced manual dexterity.

References

Smith, J. (2021). Jenny Smith Rolls on. https://jennysmithrollson.com/
The Diversity Style Guide. (2021). https://www.diversitystyleguide.com/

Chapter 6

Students with long-term medical conditions

> **Case study – Allison**
>
> Allison is a mature studying part-time. She registered on a degree in childhood and education with the intention of becoming a primary school teacher following graduation. Part way through her course, she was diagnosed with chronic fatigue syndrome (CFS), arthritis and high blood pressure. The impact her medical conditions had on her academic performance was noticeable; her fatigue left her feeling exhausted much of the time, and her arthritis was painful, particularly when sitting down for long periods. Both these conditions caused her to miss several vital teaching sessions. In addition to this, she would regularly miss further days at university because of hospital appointments. After speaking with her course tutors, and in liaison with the university's disability support staff, it was arranged that she should be allowed to miss sessions if the cause of her absence was disability related, and that she have the option to request catch-up sessions from her tutors. Given the extra time it now takes to complete assignments, she was given the option to request extensions. It was also arranged that when lectures were recorded she could access these on the VLE instead of coming onto campus. As her course also involved group work, her tutors worked closely with Allison to ensure that other group members were aware of her medical condition and that roles were assigned appropriately to each member.

As a category of disability, 'long-term medical condition' is potentially one of the most complex. It is tempting to assume that the impairments affecting individuals are somehow independent of any broader socio-cultural, economic or demographic context. Or that the intersection between condition and disablement is only understood through the social model lens of disability. While the social model does provide a solid foundation upon which to base reasonable adjustments, the impetus for supporting students with medical needs requires a nuanced appreciation of the multiple factors contributing to their disability.

Combined risk factors play their part in the possible causes of ill-health with smoking, drinking, substance misuse, poor diet or engaging in risky activities all increasing the likelihood of poor health. A further complication is the often-overlooked inter-relationship between multiple conditions, with one condition regularly affecting another. For example, while a person's economic and social status can directly impact their health, their age combined with social circumstances can exacerbate this. Of the estimated 15 million people in the UK with long-term medical conditions, about 58% are over the age of the 60 and about 14% are under 40 (The King Fund, 2022). Yet, 'the age at which people are acquiring multiple conditions is falling. People living in the most disadvantaged communities can expect to have two or more conditions ten years earlier than those in the least deprived' (Stafford et al., 2018). Universities by their very nature are populated with students from diverse cultural, economic and social backgrounds. This means that for students with chronic, long-term or multiple conditions, the support that best suits them will be driven as much by their own personal context as it is their respective conditions (Stacey, 2020). If we take as an example type 1 diabetes, it is possible to research the condition bio-medically ('where the body's immune system attacks and destroys the cells that produce insulin' according to the NHS (2021)) as well as how to manage it ('Managing blood glucose, as well as blood pressure and cholesterol, can help prevent the health problems that can occur', says the National Institute of Diabetes and Digestive and Kidney Diseases (2022)). But supporting a student with diabetes requires more than responding to the disease. People living in deprived areas and from low-income households are statistically more likely to experience long-term mental health conditions such as depression. In this case, a diabetic student from a less affluent area may be more prone to experience some of the severe symptoms associated with their diabetes if their depression worsens and they stop taking their medication. This potentially has a cyclical affect as poor diabetes control can aggravate depression leading to a particularly unhealthy inter-relationship between mental and physical health. As this single example shows, health inequality is complex and not something that can be reduced to easy simplifications; however, while making sense of this complexity may not be possible, understanding why personal health is so diverse will at least enable you to put measures in place that are responsive to individual needs. A good starting point is knowing how to make sense of medical evidence.

How to read medical evidence

Medical evidence comes in many formats. Sometimes, it can be as simple as a GP note confirming the diagnosis of a certain condition; other times, it can be a specialist consultant's report detailing a student's complete medical history. Other medical and health-related professionals can provide students with some form of evidence to confirm their conditions. It is not unusual for letters, notes, reports and even prescriptions to be provided that have been written by nurse practitioners, physiotherapists, occupational therapists, psychiatrists and pharmacists to name a few. You will need to be very clear on what your institutional policy is on what can and cannot be accepted as evidence of a long-term medical condition. If your institution holds to the policy that disability support can only begin once suitable evidence has been provided, then what constitutes 'suitable' evidence needs to be clearly understood. Again, complexity is the key word here; is the evidence recent? If not at what point does medical evidence become obsolete? (Clarke et al., 2006). Alternatively, is the condition likely to improve and clear up during the student's time studying? This is especially relevant for mid- to long-term injuries that may impact an individual for longer than 12 months but are not expected to be chronic for much longer. Is there more than one condition, in which case can one reasonable adjustment cover multiple conditions or are you responding to each diagnosis separately? For instance, if 25% additional time for exams is the standard adjustment for a student with CFS, then will another student with both CFS and anxiety-induced asthma require 50%?

Age

How old is the student? Long-term medical conditions are more prevalent in older people, which is of relevance for those institutions prioritising widening access for mature students or upskilling postgraduates. Students of all ages can present with any condition, but some conditions such as cancer, arthritis, cataracts, diabetes, osteoporosis and hypertension for example, are more common within older age brackets. This means reviewing and amending adjustments regularly. Moreover, some conditions, treatments and mortality rates are also age-related. While cancer may be more prevalent in older people, certain cancers such as melanoma, breast cancer, lymphomas (non-Hodgkin and Hodgkin) and germ cell tumours are more common amongst younger people. Again, knowing the age of the student will give some indication of the severity of their condition, any potential disruption caused by their treatment and what sort of amendments may be required in the future.

Date of evidence

How old is the evidence? Some medical reports dating back several years to early or mid-childhood may not contain much useful information with which to inform a support plan. If the student had been treated for a condition that has since fallen into remission, then the substance of the evidence may be difficult to apply today. If the evidence is too old, then some of the information contained within may have the potential to harm the individual if taken at face value. Greene et al. (2019) question whether medical evidence should come with an expiration date as it is 'not unusual for accepted therapies to be abandoned in the face of new evidence'. Their point is that some therapies previously supported by strong evidence may in time be proven to be less efficacious than previously supposed.

Multiple diagnoses?

For students living with multiple conditions, considerable attention should be given to how to respond. It is highly probable that the medical evidence will include several documents, each containing different details of multiple conditions. Given that typically medical evidence focuses on single long-term medical conditions, the decision facing university staff is whether to respond to each condition individually or take a holistic approach. It should be paramount that discussions with students occur as early as possible as many may assume a holistic approach is the right way to support them, while others may assume support options are aligned with the number of diagnoses. As people can experience different combinations of symptoms, it is important that possible fluctuations and complexities are anticipated. For example, often people affected by multiple health conditions are prescribed numerous medications for prolonged periods. Side effects of multiple medications may impact on physical bearing, mood, mental health and general wellbeing. Furthermore, for people with a complex array of health conditions, their prescriptions could change over time. To that end, scheduling regular reviews of the student's support plan is advisable if there is a good chance their overall health plan will be updated or amended. Some students may increase or decrease their medication dosage, which could take several weeks to level out. In the interim, it would be best to know what the possible effects will be (fatigue, sickness, brain fog, etc.), how long they might last and if other medication also prescribed will similarly induce negative effects.

Fluctuating conditions

Sometimes, fluctuations can be predictable, especially if changes to a student's symptoms are induced at specific times of the year or exacerbated under certain conditions, but other times, they may be wholly unpredictable and almost impossible to self-manage. It may not be possible to discern a complete health profile of the student from their medical evidence, so determining the frequency and severity of symptoms will probably not be immediately obvious. Again, detailed discussions with the student should help furnish your understanding of their condition and symptoms, as well help determine how to respond to their changing support needs. A student whose physical mobility is more restricted during winter months, for example, may need to be scheduled in accessible teaching rooms or be recommended allowances made for missed sessions. Similarly, students who live with serious illnesses such as cancer and HIV may develop associated symptoms of fatigue or depression as they progress through their studies.

Moreover, a condition can be induced to fluctuate under certain circumstances. Students with allergies may experience anaphylactic shock, the severity of which can not only be debilitating in the short term but may require long-term self-management. In such instances, any support or inclusion plan must take account of the necessity of their self-management plan and how to respond in the event of anaphylaxis. Firstly, the nature of the allergy must be determined – in other words, what are the main allergy triggers? These could be certain foods, medications or insect stings (particularly bee stings) or some fabrics. Secondly, an emergency intervention plan must be included detailing the sequence of steps needed to be taken if the student suffers a reaction. This should include describing the main symptoms so they can be identified as soon as possible, determining whether the student has an adrenaline auto-injector/epipen, along with instructions on how to use it, and instructions to either move the student away from the source of the reaction or move the source of the reaction away from the student. Apart from the emergency plan, other adjustments to help with the student's longer-term self-management can also be considered. Providing information on campus food services, menus and locations will help inform the student about potential trigger points, as will providing information on local shops where specialist diets may be purchased. If the student has chosen to live in shared accommodation or halls of residence, then it must be stressed that although recommendations for avoiding certain foods can be made to fellow students, there is no requirement or obligation for them to be taken on board. Ensuring that students with allergies are provided with their own storage space and utensils is an appropriate adjustment, as is working closely with facilities and cleaning staff to make sure that any cleaning products that could trigger a reaction are avoided.

Understanding the academic impact of long-term medical conditions

If you have been presented with only medical evidence, then health impacts upon the student's academic development may not be immediately apparent. Exploring what we can call the lived experience is vitally important as it will enable you to better understand how the student will need to adjust to university and what adjustments the university will need to make to adjust to the student.

If you are working closely with the student, then there are several areas with which to focus.

- **What is the effect on their ability to interact?** Often people living with sensitive medical conditions or experiencing long-term (possibly fluctuating) symptoms find that their social networks have gradually reduced. This may be by choice, especially if it is felt that some form of social taboo is attached to their illness or condition, or it might be because of physical debilitation, low energy and fatigue. These can impact on their time at university not just in terms of their physical capacity to engage in group work or take part in class projects but also their ability and willingness to participate in the social side of university life.
- **Are there unwritten effects?** Unwritten effects can include such factors as mental health issues that arise out of the daily efforts that come with self-management or living with chronic illness. Other effects that may be implied or stated outright in the medical evidence are whether the student will need to attend regular hospital or doctor's appointments. With such cases, allowances for missed teaching sessions will need to be made, as will the opportunity for the student to both catch up and either be granted or apply for extended deadlines for assignments. Other unwritten effects will not appear so obviously, namely the impact the student's health may have on their immediate support network or family. For students still living with family or for those with children and dependents, the collective strain of dealing with serious long-term illness can take its toll. It may be common for some students at certain times of the year to prioritise their family. Understanding their broader domestic situation is important but will probably need to be carefully deduced from the substance of the medical evidence along with conversations with the student.
- **Are there additional risk factors?** As mentioned, some conditions such as allergies can be induced because of very specific triggers. Yet, in many cases, attendant risk factors can be less easily identified, but nonetheless anticipated. For example, some lifestyle factors are known to increase the risk of or exacerbate ill-health. These range from obesity, heavy and binge drinking, smoking, substance misuse, lack of exercise, risky sexual practices and poor diet. Certainly, it is not the role of the university to monitor or regulate anyone's lifestyle choices, so should any of these activities be brought up at all, it must be done so sensitively and non-oppressively. Given the extreme sensitivity of even discussing additional risk factors, care must be given as to how you choose to broach the subject or make suggestions for additional support. If we take as an example students living with epilepsy, we can see that for many treatments, there will be attendant problems associated with lifestyle choices. Although, for instance, a Ketogenic diet (a diet high in fats and low in

carbohydrates and protein) can help some epileptics regulate their brain chemistry, such a diet is linked with health risks such as heart disease and diabetes. This particular diet, however, is not so recommended now because of other more effective medical treatments like anti-epileptic drugs (AEDs), the side effects of which can cause fatigue, lack of energy, agitation and concentration difficulties to name a few. Where additional risk factors are of relevance is when the student acts or behaves in ways likely to minimise the efficacy of their treatment. This means that although alcohol can be consumed in modest amounts, 'moderate to heavy drinking over a short space of time can make you more likely to have a seizure' (Epilepsy Action, 2022). Regulating drinking habits, dietary requirements and physical activity may not directly be within the purview of the university, but there must nonetheless be a requirement to ensure university staff can provide their students with enough information to inform their lifestyle choices and access advice and guidance when it is needed.

Difficulties the student may experience

It would be impossible to list the number of medical conditions students may live with. It would similarly be impossible to estimate the possible symptoms of those conditions or the frequency with which they might occur with any accuracy. Bearing this in mind, what follows is a general breakdown of many of the difficulties students with long-term medical conditions may experience, but it is not by any means an exhaustive list. University staff are therefore advised to consider with caution what a student's medical evidence reveals as in many cases the information will need to be inferred or discussed sensitively with the student.

Students in this case absolutely must be central to the decision-making process. Early communication is important here as it is important to manage expectations early. Therefore, be secure in your own knowledge early on as to the limits of your own role to either recommend or put in place adjustments. Here are some tips:

- **Irregular attendance**. Students with long-term medical conditions not only miss out on educational activities but are far more likely to fall behind with their studies. Regularly occurring absenteeism has been linked not only to reduced academic achievement but also to social disengagement alienation (Johnson, 2005; Gottfried, 2014, 2019).
- **Periods when they are unable to study**. This can include times when their conditions flare up to the extent that any form of academic engagement is seriously limited, or when they must attend important medical appointments. Whatever the reason, it is recommended that if students' attendance will vary, then this is acknowledged and communicated to all

relevant university departments. For those institutions that closely monitor student engagement, much unnecessary stress and anxiety can be avoided if it is recorded that there are legitimate medical reasons to explain their absence. Moreover, even if their attendance has not been affected, access to teaching does not in itself mean inclusion. There may be many reasons for this: fatigue, medication side effects, physical discomfort, for example. This of course means that if their full engagement with the teaching is hindered because of their health, then it follows that so will their ability to study independently outside of scheduled teaching times.

- **Deteriorating condition**. Not all medical conditions or health problems present with a fixed set of symptoms. Some cancers, arthritis, multiple sclerosis, muscular dystrophy for example can progress over time. The effects of which can limit students' engagement academically, prompt feelings of isolation, make worse any pain or discomfort they experience and place further strain on their and their immediate support network's emotional wellbeing. It also means that while a support and inclusion plan might perfectly suit a student's needs one year, additional adjustments will need to be put in place later on.
- **Stamina problems**. Restricted stamina will regularly impact on students' academic progress. This is not quite the same as living with a fluctuating condition, but there are similarities, not least when students may be at their most optimal and when they might be at their most limited. It would be worth exploring with students early on when they are at their most energised. For some, they may be perfectly capable of full engagement until at a certain point in the day, whereupon energy levels may dip, fatigue sets in, physical symptoms flare up or the effects of the medication kicks in. Evening classes, out-of-hours group work, exam revision and even just studying may be particularly difficult for the student under such circumstances.
- **Past medical history may have led to gaps in their education**. We have already acknowledged that for some students with long-term medical conditions their attendance may fluctuate as a direct result of their health. We must presume, then, for some students, this has been a feature of their educational experiences throughout their lives. If so, we cannot know for sure whether there are gaps in their education, how these may affect their ability to adapt to a higher education environment or what additional services on top of reasonable adjustments may be required. Missing a lot of pre-university education because of ill-health can substantially impact not just academic development but also their general attitude to formal education. Missed schooling can affect their self-confidence, sometimes causing students to become anxious about registering on their course. Even if the student's condition is in remission or they have been clear of their illness for some time, nonetheless they may still be disadvantaged if their formative experiences included a serious disruption of their education.

- **Anxiety about disclosing their condition.** We shall explore the sensitivities surrounding the taboo of illness and health in the following chapter. But for now, we cannot ignore the fact that personal health is not simply a problem that applies to education. It is an incredibly emotive area for many people, and one that may be difficult to broach without some difficulty. For some students, it may not occur to them that there is even the option to not only disclose their medical condition but also have adjustments made because of it. For others, they may be fully aware of the help they are entitled to but choose initially not to disclose for personal reasons. Such reasons may include concerns about being discriminated against or otherwise differentiated; a determination to work through their illness as best they can without any support; or simply to avoid yet another health review. We must not forget that for so many students being at university is an incredibly liberating time, at once more independent than they have ever been before and given more personal agency to determine their own lived experiences. We should not be surprised if students, having been subjected to a barrage of medical interventions over the years, choose not to go through the whole thing all over again.

Working with students – creating a support plan

Remember, a student's personal health is unique to them. Identifying common symptoms and general features of this diagnosis or that disease will tell you something about the physical aspect of their health but not everything. A long-term health condition is something that will affect an individual's life on multiple levels. This means that although researching the symptoms of, for example, epilepsy or IBS may inform your recommendations for adjustments to some extent, you must also consider that to many their illness and health isn't something they have but is something that makes them who they are. Their lives, lifestyle and sense if personal identity may be bound to their health, which is understandable if it has been a driving force of much of their daily experiences.

- **Focus on the student as the central figure in the inclusion plan.** Ensure the student's voice is heard. Give them the opportunity to explain their previous experiences, what their concerns are for the future and what support they feel they will need. They are the true experts in themselves, so it would be remiss to overlook the wealth of information they can provide about the impact of their health upon their lives and academic development.
- **Explore the student's expectations of support.** Be sure what your institution may or may not do. An example of this is whether there is anyone who can help the student with their medication. Some students arriving at a university may have previously had experiences in school/college where their education providers arranged for medical treatments

to be done on site. This is something that is not necessarily guaranteed within a university, so if medication assistance is expected, communicate quickly how far the institution can help. Equally, there may be no expectation for such interventionist assistance, but nonetheless there might be the suggestion that a private and discreet place is made available for students to use for their medical treatment.
- **Ask the student to detail examples of their previous support.** Previous support provisions might not have occurred to you if your only understanding of the student's possible needs is derived only from their medical evidence. Students with certain medical conditions may have previously been permitted different exam adjustments than you had anticipated. Rest breaks, permission to take medication into the exam hall or a room on their own if other students are permitted to bring with them food and drink are all possible adjustments.
- **Will their medical condition affect their social life?** As many institutions market themselves as much for the social life as the academic quality of the degrees, exploring whether students will have difficulty accessing this aspect of higher education is not an irrelevant line of enquiry. Make available a list of what clubs, societies, etc. are on offer. What does the student enjoy doing normally? Is there a danger that their health may cause social isolation? Discuss about making friends, when some activities take place, e.g., many take place on evenings and weekends, but others might be online or flexibly moveable. Also, if the student is intent on living as independently as possible, provide them with information about local cafes, friendly bars, along with their opening times.
- **Enquire about the student's living arrangements**. If living at home (their family home), would they prioritise developing a social life at university, or is this something the university can advise on? If they are residing in student accommodation, will they need additional support with storing medication, scheduled check calls, a PEEP? Some halls with have resident mentors or hall wardens; would the student like to introduce themselves to them and discuss their health issues? You cannot make the decision for the student, but while discussing their needs, you certainly can provide them with the option to make an informed choice.
- **What are their eating requirements?** Students with some long-term medical conditions are more likely to experience financial hardship due to various factors such as limited employment options, the expense of prescription medication or the cost of purchasing more expensive ingredients for a specialist diet. In which case, they may need advice on sourcing cheaper foods for easy meals that is nutritious and compatible with their dietary requirements. Be aware of what food options are available across the campus from the on-site canteens, refectories and cafes. Also, the student may appreciate information on local shops and suppliers of foods and ingredients, along with prices.

- **Cleaning their shared living accommodation may be disrupted if the student's health declines.** This is something that cannot be put on a support plan, but it is something that can be addressed with the student and from there engage with housemates. Possibly via resident warden (if present), but it would be worth advising on where to obtain useful cleaning aids such as rubber gloves (or alternatives if danger of allergy), multi-purpose wipes, sponges on sticks, grabber tools and cordless vacuum cleaners. But also whether the student would like advice and guidance managing the expectations of their fellow housemates if their health causes a noticeable decline in their ability to share domestic responsibilities.
- **Ask if the student has or requires a PA to help with everyday living.** Ask how fellow students would wish to be alerted to their presence.
- **Shared bathroom – does student have or need their own bathroom?** If so, will this be better for mobility aids and grab handles? A student with their own bathroom will be put at less risk of cross-contamination from other people's cosmetic products and provide some much needed privacy in case bathroom related discretion is required.
- **Discuss disclosure and confidentiality.** Can a support or inclusion plan be created without the need to include details of the student's illness or diagnosis? How much information is the student willing to share and with whom? Think about how to share the information, especially if there is a likelihood of multiple copies of the support plan being distributed.
- **Extended deadlines; clarify with student the university policy.** Some institutions can automatically grant blanket extensions, other may have different policy. If it is believed that an extension is necessary as otherwise there is a risk of discrimination and unfair treatment, then it should be insisted that an extension is awarded.

References

Clark, M., Donovan, E.F. and Schoettker, P. (June 2006). From outdated to updated, keeping clinical guidelines valid. *International Journal for Quality in Health Care*, 18(3), pp. 165–166.

Epilepsy Action (2022). https://www.epilepsy.org.uk/?gclid=-Cj0KCQjw4omaBhDqARIsADXULuVmXoT1lVvnLdkrvxe-c_X-RGd3tb8nl2RxjyTFUueOpNYy9eEfpbgaAhdoEALw_wcB

Gottfried, M.A. (2014). Chronic absenteeism and its effects on students' academic and socioemotional outcomes. *Journal of Education for Students Placed at Risk (JESPAR)*, 19(2), pp. 53–75.

Gottfried, M.A. (2019). Chronic absenteeism in the classroom context. *Urban Education*, 54(1), pp. 1–34.

Greene, P., Prasad, V. and Cifu, A. (2019). Should evidence come with an expiration date?. *Journal of General Internal Medicine*, 34(7), pp. 1356–1357.

Kings Fund. (2022). https://www.kingsfund.org.uk/
National Health Service (NHS). (2021). Diabetes. https://www.nhs.uk/conditions/diabetes/
National Institute of Diabetes and Digestive and Kidney Diseases. (2022). https://www.niddk.nih.gov/
Stacey, P. (2020). *University and chronic illness: A survival guide.* Daisa & Co.
Stafford, M., Steventon, A., Thorlby, R., Fisher, R., Turton, C. and Deeny, S. (2018). *Understanding the health care needs of people with multiple health conditions.* Health Foundation.

Chapter 7

Disability, illness and taboo

Case study – Xuesong

Xuesong arrived in the UK from China. He had registered at university to study a postgraduate degree in economics and business management. While studying at university, he began to experience problems consistent with anxiety and depression: demotivation, low energy levels and prolonged periods of procrastination. Many of his friends also noticed he was becoming increasingly withdrawn and sullen. Xuesong initially chose not to avail himself of his university's support service, fearing that this would affect both his reputation as a capable student and his career prospects. Eventually, his personal tutor decided to speak with him following several weeks of disengagement and very obvious signs of distress. She assured him that if he needed support, the university could provide this discreetly and confidentially. He was put in touch with the university's mental health service who, following an initial assessment, recommended some talking therapy. Xuesong was given the option to access this support from a mental health professional who was also a Chinese speaker if that helped. Meanwhile, his disability service department liaised closely with his academic department to recommend adjustments, including extra time in exams, extensions for coursework assignments and the option to request alternative assessments for presentations.

Understanding diverse attitudes to illness, disease and disability

Between 1990 and 1994, the African state of Rwanda fell into a brutal and bloody civil war. The conflict was the culmination of a long-running dispute that had existed between the Hutu and Tutsi groups within Rwandan society, a dispute that had been raging for many decades following the country's independence. It was fought primarily between the Rwandan Armed Forces, representing the government, and the rebel Rwandan Patriotic Front (RPF). The Rwandan army represented the Hutu-dominated government, who during the Rwandan Revolution of 1959–1961 deposed and replaced the minority Tutsi monarchy and endeavoured from there to displace many leading political and influential Tutsis. Of the three main ethnic groups in Rwanda (Hutu, Tutsi and Twa), the Hutus were by far the largest, with the Tutsis being second largest and the Twa the smallest. Following the overthrow of the Tutsi monarchy, many thousands of Tutsis were then forced into exile within neighbouring African countries such as Uganda, where eventually rebel groups such as the Rwandan Patriotic Force were formed. On October the first 1990, the RPF invaded the north-east of the country, precipitating one of, if not the most, the violent and deadly wars of the twentieth century.

Numbers vary, but it has been estimated that about 5 million people lost their lives during the Rwandan civil war with over 40% of the population having been killed or fled the country to escape the violence. By 1994, a treaty had eventually been brokered and agreed, bringing an end to the tragic conflict.

Why is this relevant? It is relevant because of what happened afterwards when international aid agencies, NGOs and humanitarian charities descended upon Rwanda with the intention of helping and supporting the blighted population. Given the sheer scale of the brutality, it was understandably assumed that incidences of psychological trauma would need to be addressed as a matter of urgency. Western experts, equipped with their specialist knowledge and training in PTSD and therapeutic interventions, soon set to providing a range of mental health support for victims of the war. However, not all went according to plan. In the immediate aftermath of the war, it soon became apparent there existed very different notions about the best way to treat mental health disorders. Adopting a primarily clinical approach to care, western mental health experts failed to consider the possible cultural differences that existed between the providers of the care and those on the receiving end of it. While researching different cultural conceptions of mental health and depression, Andrew Solomon made the point following discussions with Rwandan aid workers that western aid workers were intrusive and offensive in their approach to support, with many Rwandans feeling that the western clinical practice imposed upon them actually had the opposite effect of what had been intended. Rather than helping to heal people from the psychological damage of conflict, their approach instead served to retraumatise them. As he pointed out:

> Their practice did not involve being outside in the sun where you begin to feel better. There was no music or drumming to get your blood flowing again. There was no sense that everyone had taken the day off so that the entire community could come together to try to lift you up and bring you back to joy. Instead, they would take people one at a time into these dingy

little rooms and have them sit around for an hour or so and talk about bad things that had happened to them. We had to ask them to leave.

(Leach, 2015)

What this illustrates is the ease with which it is possible to fall into a belief system that no matter how commonsensical or seemingly rational can nonetheless be easily undone by an alternative perspective. One may have no reason to assume that something as relatively straight forward as understanding depression can be so comprehensively confounded by the social and cultural circumstances of a person whose background differs from our own. And yet Solomon, in his bestselling book *The Noonday Demon*, observed that 'monolithic problem of depression cannot be addressed with a monolithic response; depressions are contextual and must be interpreted within the contexts in which they occur' (Solomon, 2002: 135).

Equally, the same is true of most illnesses, diseases and disabilities. The image of international, predominantly western aid, agencies providing culturally inappropriate support to the Rwandan victims of genocide is an extreme but not unique example of misaligned expectations when it comes to health support. And higher education is no exception. The past several years have seen attempts by many universities to widen the participation of students from across society, often through rigorous international recruitment. This of course means the potential for divergent perspectives on disability, mental health, illness and any attendant taboos attached to those beliefs. Therefore, if increasing numbers of students enter higher education with diverse notions of disability, then it follows that there will be a significant number of students with different ideas about disability support. Providing culturally sensitive support means more than awareness raising or being open to discussion about alternative notions of disability. While acknowledging the lived experiences of people from other cultural, racial, religious or national backgrounds is important, so is reflecting upon your own expectations about the students whom you are meant to be supporting. As professionals, it is incumbent on us all to realise the importance of being informed around the 'rich and diverse array of beliefs, expectations, preferences, and behavioural make up of the social cultures' (Hammoud et al., 2005: 1307) that constitute the student body.

Concepts of health and disability

Support services have finite resources with which to respond to students' needs, which means coordinating the delivery of reasonable adjustments is a task that necessarily must take on board multiple variables. These, of course, range from the nature of the student's disability, the likely impact their conditions may have upon their studies, to what potentially disabling educational elements need to be adjusted and whether certain courses are more or less equipped to handle those adjustments. In addition to all of these is the cultural element.

Students' lived experiences are complex and diverse; they will all have their own unique personal experiences, with many students experiencing multiple forms of discrimination and exclusion. As well as disability, it is important to consider everything else that can potentially marginalise students. Issues of gender, race, class and sexual orientation are all important areas for consideration, as are crucially how those personal experiences have informed their views on what support is and the reasons for it.

Examples of intersectional discrimination are not hard to find and often consist of professional biases (sometimes conscious, sometimes not) that regularly result in poorer qualities of care. In 2002 in the US, the Institute for Medicine's Unequal Treatment: Confronting Racial and Ethnic Disparities in Health Care, stated that 'Racial and ethnic minorities tend to receive a lower quality of health care than non-minorities...', with Hammoud et al. (2005) responding that one reason for such inequitable treatment lies in the absence of cultural training for healthcare providers. Their point is that 'unintentional violation of customs, rituals, or deeply held beliefs can prevent the establishment of relationships that allow healthcare providers to begin exploring important issues with patients from different cultures' (2005: 1308). There is no reason to assume that much the same cannot be applied in the UK to higher education disability support. The UK/western university model is, like the US and UK healthcare system, accustomed to emphasising the individual and their needs. The prevalent belief is that once a student is registered on their course, then their immediate family and life outside university is of limited concern to the institution. Although there is a growing acceptance of the significant role of family in people's lives, with provision for staff/student childcare or allowances made for the care of relatives, the fundamental belief is with the sanctity of the individual. This is, in one very fundamental way, a political and philosophical belief, one borne from years of western cultural evolution pivoting from religious and social collectivism to more secular notions of individual freedoms. Despite louder calls for parents or family members to play a greater role in their children's academic inclusion, the general position within universities is that parents and family members should be excluded as much as possible, with the greatest emphasis placed on individual student development. While this is justified for all sorts of reasons (data protection, confidentiality, encouraging independent learning), it can and does frame disability support within the kind of western model we saw earlier in Rwanda. By degrees of policy and tradition, it misses the vital importance that some cultures place in the family's role of treating illness or caring for a member with additional needs. In which case, it is not a rhetorical question to ask what is being missed with the support universities provide? By orienting support towards a fully independent, autonomous student and then procedures surrounding confidentiality, disclosure and informed consent may overlook certain cultural preferences around how students self-identify as relative to rather than independent of their families.

University staff, in other words, may put measures in place to barrier off family members from support, but in doing so, miss the possibility that other decisions around healthcare management are being addressed elsewhere. Of course, in this cultural and social context, disclosure also works both ways; it has been noted for example that an individual not usually identified as disabled in the developed world may be considered disabled in many societies if they are unable to participate in important life activities (Devlieger, 1995; Banks et al., 1989; Zhang and Bennett, 2001) such as childbearing or contributing to family income. In our increasingly pluralistic and multicultural educational environment, people make sense of their disability by drawing upon their cultural beliefs and values (Stromquist, 2006), meaning that there will always be the potential for a breakdown in trust between the student, their immediate family and the institution if not appropriately addressed (Lamorey, 2002; Skinner and Weisner, 2007). Again, it would be unwise to slip into erroneous assumptions about a perceived western/non-western dichotomy of cultures. For every example of a supposed cultural difference, it will not be hard to find a corresponding example. Continuing with the role of the family and wider social sphere in the lived experience of disabled students, we can easily find parallel examples. In Chapter 5, we explored support for students with physical impairments, which included the role of the care giver. If your institution already has a process in place to provide students with the option to include a care giver of their choice, then this is something that should be made optional for all students for whatever reason.

Understanding broader cultural issues is similarly vital. For some students, fasting rituals are an important aspect of their faith. Buddhism, Christianity, Islam, Judaism, Taoism, Jainism and Hinduism all practice fasting. Fasting varies across and within religions, can variously last days or weeks and involves the deliberate refrainment of food and drink, usually during the day. For students with medical conditions or long-term treatment plans, the effects of fasting on their overall health can be serious, and although allowances are made in most religions for medications and sustenance to be taken during the fast, it is worth ensuring that students are given the option to disclose if their treatment plans will be affected during this period. For students without the need to medicate, fasting can still exacerbate already existing difficulties. A student with a specific learning difficulty, for example, may already experience difficulties with cognitive functioning, which can be amplified during the fasting period. Alsharidah et al. (2016) concluded in their study on the effects of fasting during the holy month of Ramadan that 'fasting is associated with significant changes in cognition, and causes a drop in diastolic blood pressure in healthy subjects'. The significance of their findings for fasting students is that their ability to study will be compromised the longer it continues, meaning greater cognitive dysfunction for students already experiencing reduced ability in areas of executive functioning.

While being sensitive to cultural practices is important when considering the needs of the student, so is sensitivity to much broader concepts of health and disability. As mentioned, in the west, there is a prevalent belief that matters pertaining to health and general wellbeing are centred around the individual, with family and community as somewhat peripheral to this. But, it would be presumptuous to adopt this position for all students. It is not uncommon for students to consider disability as something of a cultural taboo, with some societies using expressions that signify oppression and exclusion in their daily parlance (Eyben et al., 2008) or embed policies and practices that result in a 'loss of freedom to exercise choice about the lives' they wish to lead (Munsaka and Charnley, 2013: 762). But again, it would be wrong to take the position that some societies are more progressive than others; in the Introduction, we saw how negative cultural attitudes to disability in the UK are still commonplace and often draw upon cultural, religious and sociological misconceptions about disability. What is needed, therefore, is preparation for all concerned to negotiate both the transition into higher education for disabled students, and even the extent to which disabled students choose to identify as disabled themselves. Nicolaisen makes the point that

> we can deal scientifically and practically with disability only if we are sensitive to the cultural, social and psychological structures in which it is embedded. Every culture poses a challenge to preconceived notions and forces us to ask anew disability is understood, conceptualised and dealt with.
>
> (1995: 39)

Writing a culturally sensitive support plan

Firstly, it would not be possible to identify all the potential cultural elements needed to write a culturally sensitive support plan. Nonetheless, acknowledging the diversity of existing experiences, attitudes, values and beliefs amongst the student population is a good starting point.

- **Reflect on you own cultural beliefs**: If you are employed in a university disability service, student support department or are part of the academic staff, you may have preconceived notions about what disability is or is not. Many of the barriers facing disabled university students may be socially derived, with negative attitudes, conscious or otherwise, playing their part in their marginalisation. Ask yourself what you know about disability, what your previous experiences have been and if you are familiar with relevant legislation such as the Equality Act 2010. Ask yourself:
- **Do you know what is covered by disability according to the Equality Act 2010?**
- **Have you heard of the social model or the medical model of disability?**

- **Where has your understanding of disability mostly derived?** For example, cultural representations? Personal experience? Professional capacity?
- **Do you believe most people share your notions of disability?** If so, why? If not, why?
- For those already working in a student support or disability service, it is not advisable to assume that you are better informed than a colleague who does not specialise in this area. We have already seen from the Rwanda example that concepts of disability, even the meaning of the word, are not culturally universal. So, if you are familiar with the Equality Act 2010, can you likewise assume that all students will 'know their rights' as you do? If you have heard of the social or medical models of disability, can you be certain that students from certain cultural or transnational backgrounds will share your belief that disability is a social construct and not a wholly medical issue, or indeed a consequence of cultural practices? Similarly, if you believe most people will share your notions of disability, then you are assuming a universal standard of understanding that does not exist.

You should by now be aware that how we think about disability is not without complications. You may, therefore, benefit by endeavouring to compartmentalise the main elements of disability and diversity.

- **How diverse is your institution?** Some institutions are more diverse than others, with many HEIs making a point of recruiting students more locally while others prefer to tap into the international market. Likewise, many universities actively engage in promoting their institutions to students from ethnic minority backgrounds while others are perhaps not so inclined. Whatever your own institution's policy check to see what the cultural makeup is, data should be available from your admissions department. Explore the data to see the percentage of student diversity and, if possible, match against the number of students accessing disability support. Much here depends on your willingness to crunch the numbers, so make life easier for yourself by beginning with broad strokes. Assume that about 15%–20% of any given population will be disabled. Firstly, does this number generally apply to your institution? Secondly, can this number be granulated further to include students from across the university? In other words, is about the same amount of male or female student registering as disabled? Are mature or part-time students similarly represented? And of course, is this base-level percentage reflected across students from ethnic minatory backgrounds, international students or students who are practicing their religions? If not, then you will need to ask why. Keeping accurate, up-to-date records will swiftly enable you to identify which groups of students are more or less likely to disclose a disability and, crucially, access support.
- **How well is disability awareness promoted throughout your institution?** If your university takes active measures to promote disability

awareness, be sure to take account of how people perceive disability differently from one another. This is necessary if your institution has a high proportion of international students, with English as a second language. 'Disability' may have slightly different meanings or connotations to some students, and it cannot be discounted that certain taboos associated with disability could prevent students from seeking support. Moreover, if the full range of disability inclusion is not promoted, then for all students, irrespective or their cultural backgrounds, they may not realise support is available to them.

- **Do you assess language comprehension/provide interpreters?** Taking account of the potential for language difficulties is worth considering. Even if language proficiency is high, students should be provided with the opportunity to discuss whether an interpreter would be of benefit. As mentioned previously, where there may be divergent understandings around notions of informed consent, then an interpreter may be able to act as an intermediary. And again, this is not something that should be considered for students only from international or ethnic minority backgrounds. It has previously been mentioned that many students arrive at university with care workers or support staff who often act as their advocate. There is no reason why the same cannot be applied for all students who may need a third party. Certainly, this would not be thought of as an unreasonable adjustment for a student whose first language is BSL, so it should likewise be considered completely reasonable elsewhere. The benefits of an interpreter are that they may filter important, subjective information between staff/student. But it is important to determine if the interpreter is sufficiently fluent in medical, educational and disability terminology. As with a BSL interpreter, work with the language interpreter/intermediary by explaining key concepts, specialist terminology and key policies.
- **Consider gender preference:** Here, we must be careful. Some students from particular cultural or religious backgrounds may agree to speak about private health matters with university staff but prefer for that discussion to be with someone of a specific gender. Here, we must be careful not to confuse sensitivity to individual needs with direct gender discrimination. Discretion must be exercised here, so take time to evaluate the situation to determine whether the preference is reasonable. For the most part, it probably will be.
- **Use culturally sensitive language for support plans:** If you need to remove the word 'disability' from any support plan, do so. Also (and again this applies to all students), be aware of the sensitive nature of the student's disability, medical condition or learning difficulty. It may be that they have tentatively agreed to discuss support, but that their condition may be fundamentally private to them. In which case, draft a version of the plan that the student is satisfied with. This may include removing all mention of their disability and even renaming the plan as something else altogether,

e.g. an inclusion plan. If there is some reluctance to mention illness, disability and health matters, then emphasise instead the recommended adjustments as educational matters. This will deflect the attention away from any taboo or reluctance to disclose private health matters and focus instead on classroom, educational practice.

References

Alsharidah, A.M., Murtaza, G., Alsharidah, M.M. and Bashir, S. (2016). Fasting in Ramadan affects cognitive and physiological function in normal subjects (pilot study). *Neuroscience and Medicine*, 7(2), pp. 60–65.

Banks, J., Banks, C. and Banks, M. (1989). *Multicultural education: Issues and perspectives*. Allyn & Bacon.

Devlieger, P. (1995). Why disabled? The cultural understanding of physical disability in an African society. In B. Ingstad and S. Reynolds White (eds), *Disability and Culture*. University of California Press, pp. 94–106.

Eyben, R., Kabeer, N. and Cornwall, A. (2008). Conceptualising empowerment and the implications for pro-poor growth: A paper for the DAC Poverty Network. https://www.ids.ac.uk/download.php?file=files/dmfile/conceptualisingempowermentpaperforPOVNET.pdf

Hammoud, M.M., White, C.B. and Fetters, M.D. (2005). Opening cultural doors: Providing culturally sensitive healthcare to Arab American and American Muslim patients. *American Journal of Obstetrics and Gynecology*, 193(4), pp. 1307–1311.

Lamorey, S. (2002). The effects of culture on special education services: Evil eyes, prayer meetings, and IEPs. *Teaching Exceptional Children*, 34(5), pp. 67–71.

Leach, A. (2015). Exporting trauma: Can the talking cure do more harm than good? The Guardian, 5 February 2015. https://www.theguardian.com/global-development-professionals-network/2015/feb/05/mental-health-aid-western-talking-cure-harm-good-humanitarian-anthropologist.

Munsaka, E. and Charnley, H. (2013). We do not have chiefs who are disabled': Disability, development and culture in a continuing complex emergency. *Disability & Society*, 28(6), pp. 756–769.

Nicolaisen, I. (1995). Persons and nonpersons: Disability and personhood among the Punan Bah of central Borneo. In B. Ingstad and S.R. Whyte (eds), *Disability and Culture* (pp. 38–55). University of California Press.

Skinner, D. and Weisner, T.S. (2007). Sociocultural studies of families of children with intellectual disabilities. *Mental Retardation and Developmental Disabilities Research Reviews*, 13(4), pp. 302–312.

Solomon, A. (2002). *The noonday demon: An anatomy of depression*. Vintage.

Stromquist, N.P. (2006). Comparative and international education: A journey toward equality and equity. In B. Piper, S. Dryden-Peterson and Y. Kim (eds), *International education for the millennium: Toward access equality and equity* (pp. 15–36). Harvard University Press.

Zhang, C. and Bennett, T. (2001). *Multicultural views of disability: Implications for early intervention professionals*. Infant-Toddler Intervention.

Conclusion

Be an ally: the social model revisited

Let us revisit the social model. You may remember this from the Introduction; it is the model of disability that frames disablement within a specific social context. It states that to be disabled is to be marginalised or oppressed from one's own society rather than through any innate limitation or difference within oneself. Perhaps the defining feature of the social model of disability can be summarised as 'inclusion' – inclusion in all matters pertaining to social activity: health, housing, education and work to name a few. Leisure, relationships and independence of choice to name a few more. As progressive as the word 'inclusion' may sound, it nonetheless has a rather nebulous quality to it. What actually *is* inclusion? Is it the same as acceptance? If so acceptance by whom? And based upon what drivers or criteria do those doing the accepting determine who should or should not be included? Does inclusion more broadly mean the same as access? Accessing better health services, housing and education will surely lead to greater levels of inclusion! Perhaps. But then again, perhaps not. Simply sharing space with those for whom any given environment is their natural environment does not in itself mean that equitability has been achieved, rather that inequality has been recognised.

In a world that has been created to centre the non-disabled as the primary agents of social impetus, we may with some justification take for granted the assertion that 'majority groups have helped preserve the status quo, which favours them, by relegating diversity, equity, and inclusion efforts to human resources instead of using their own power to effect change' (Melaku et al., 2020). What this in effect means is that in many instances the failure to effect change, whether for disabled people or more widely across the diversity spectrum, lies squarely amongst those whom Melaku et al. (2020) characterise as failing 'to acknowledge their own privilege', but who nonetheless can position themselves as allies of the marginalised, which can include disabled individuals. In this regard, what this book has hopefully achieved is to guide readers towards the acknowledgement that what we call 'disability support' in higher education (and indeed across the whole of society) is not and should not be the exclusive preserve of a few specialist members of staff. Although it must be accepted that some disabled students will require specialist services at some point, the substantial role played by all staff across the institution is pivotal to the inclusion of disabled students, irrespective of their role within the university. This necessarily means being challenged on the assumptions one may hold about disability, and the possible perception that supporting disabled students is something left to others. The notion of being 'challenged', for example, is something that is often mentioned in relation to widening participation and the role students can play in bringing their personal lived experiences into a higher education setting. Naturally, every student has their own lived experience that informs their world view and frames how they respond to and make sense of their immediate environments, and this is no less true of disabled students whose world view may likely have been influenced by years of discrimination, inconvenience or marginalisation. By ensuring that students from diverse backgrounds have opportunities to challenge their education, decolonise their curricula, insist on content warnings for challenging aspects of their course or question the teaching and assessment methods in relation to their personal circumstances, we can see how an egalitarian, more pluralistic environment can emerge. And yet, in many instances, the very real-world challenges faced by disabled students in accessing their universities are often seen more as challenges for those who assume that this sort of inclusion is something best left to the support team. Recommended reasonable adjustments, to put it plainly, are only a small part of the solution. Which of course means that with every solution, there must be a problem. Still adhering to our social model of disability, we can say that the problem is not just ensuring some access is achieved but also that attitudes towards disabled people are indeed challenged and, if necessary, addressed. To assume that disabled students should only talk about their disability to a designated disability team is to hold a view that disability itself is something to be ignored if at all possible. What it says is that this vital and important part of the individual should not be openly acknowledged. What it also says is that disabled students cannot rely on some non-disabled people as allies, in the same way other historically marginalised groups can call upon support from their own majority group allies.

This raises the question as to what should an ally do exactly? Perhaps, the first thing would be to reflect upon one's own attitudes regarding disability, and whether more responsibility needs to be taken regarding the extent to which personal attitudes and beliefs may have influenced or reinforced possible prejudicial behaviours. To be an ally, therefore, is to view the concept of allyship as a 'strategic mechanism used by individuals to become collaborators, accomplices, and co-conspirators who fight injustice and promote equity … through supportive personal relationships and public acts of sponsorship and advocacy. Allies endeavour to drive systemic improvements…' (Melaku et al., 2020). Allies, of course, currently exist as supporters of marginalised or discriminated people throughout many facets of society, whether as men actively working to help reduce the negative underrepresentation of women (Moser and Branscombe, 2022) or as heterosexual individuals engaged in collective action alongside the LGBTQ community (Russell, 2011). In many cases, the pathways for such motivations can range from an awareness of the privilege that exists from members of a majority group to greater involvement in social activism more generally, to direct personal involvement with historically marginalised persons (Russell, 2011). These initial drivers all share a common theme, namely that for allies to exist, there was a moment of conscious awareness in the mind of the person choosing to be in alliance with others. There is no reason as to why the same cannot be applied to allies of disabled individuals in general and disabled students in particular.

Much, therefore, depends on encouraging non-disabled people to view 'disability' as something pertaining to social justice and civil rights, rather than something that exists wholly within the purview of specialist services. Disability in this respect becomes something that can be challenged conceptually if we think differently about the social mechanisms of exclusion and the normalisation of majority group assumptions.

When supporting disabled students in higher education, reasonable adjustments can only take us so far if we are serious about access and inclusion. Much more depends on that moment of self-awareness in recognising that university teaching and learning environments are constructs, constructs indeed that have been founded upon many years of tradition and established good practice, but constructs nonetheless that are daily challenged when confronted by the requirements of disabled students. As higher education professionals, we wish for all students to value their time at university and to come away having learned valuable lessons and skills, whether by formal teacher-led training or less formal social engagement. The very worst thing to happen is for disabled students' higher education experiences to be so negative as to solidify the belief that university isn't for them. That they have no allies, or their voices, personal experiences and lives are not relevant to all staff across the institution.

In other words, be an ally!

References

Melaku, T.M., Beeman, A., Smith, D.G. and Johnson, W.B. (2020). Be a better ally. *Harvard Business Review*, 98(6), pp. 135–139.

Moser, C.E. and Branscombe, N.R. (2022). Male allies at work: Gender-equality supportive men reduce negative underrepresentation effects among women. *Social Psychological and Personality Science*, 13(2), pp. 372–381.

Russell, G.M. (2011). Motives of heterosexual allies in collective action for equality. *Journal of Social Issues*, 67(2), pp. 376–393.

Index

Note: **Bold** page numbers refer to tables.

Abberley, P. 6
ability 3, 6, 13, 15–17, 25, 59, 63, 83, 86, 95, 113, 124
academic impact 112–114
academic quality 117
accessible recruitment practices: recruitment event/open day 67–68; registration process 67
accessible rooms 73–75
accessible routes 73–75
accommodation 112; indoor adaptations, adjustments 72; and interaction 71; outdoor adaptations, adjustments 72; physical impairments 102–103
adjustments: accommodation 71–72; room 75; teaching environment 77, 86–87; teaching spaces and acoustics 85–86
adrenaline auto-injector/epipen 112
Adreon, D. 25
age 110
agoraphobia **45–46**
aid communication 86
alcohol consumption 114
Algorta, G.P. 51
Allison case 108
Amy case 38–39
anaphylactic shock 112
anaphylaxis 112
anti-epileptic drugs (AEDs) 114
anxiety disorder 116; agoraphobia **45–46**; body dysmorphic disorder **45**; categories 42–46; generalised anxiety disorder **42**; health anxiety (hypochondria) **45**; mental and physical affects 41–42; panic attacks/disorder **43**; post-traumatic stress disorder **44**; social anxiety disorder **43**
arthritis 96, 97, 108, 115
Asperger's/Asperger syndrome 23, 24
atomoxetine 20, **22**
attention deficit hyperactivity disorder (ADHD): accessing resources 33; assessments (accessible/alternative) 33; course delivery 32; course design 31; definition 18–20; hyperactive-impulsive 18, **19**; inattentive 18, **19**; symptoms 18; treatment 20, **21–22**
autism: accessing resources 33–34; assessments (accessible/alternative) 34–36; case study 23; course delivery 32–33; course design 31–32; definition 23; extreme anxiety 26; highly focused interests or hobbies 26; medical classification 23–24; meltdowns and shutdowns 26; under or over-sensitivity 26; repetitive and restrictive behaviour 26; social communication challenges 25; social interaction challenges 25
autism spectrum condition (ASC) 23
autism spectrum disorder (ASD) 23

barriers to learning: physical spaces 26–27; sensory factors 27, **27–28**
Barry case 12–13
Beale-Ellis, S. 6
behavioural symptoms: depressive episodes **50**; manic episodes **48–49**
Belser, J.W. 7
Berlin, R. 13

bipolar disorder: definition 48; depressive episodes **50**; manic episodes **48–49**; primary characteristics **48–50**
blurred/cloudy vision 63
body dysmorphic disorder **45**
Bond, J. 1
British Council of Organisations of Disabled People (BCODP) 5
British Dyslexia Association (BDA) 14
British Sign Language (BSL) 86
broader cultural issues 124
Buddhism faith 124

Cai, R. Y. 25
campus food services 112
cancers 82, 110, 112, 115
care workers: accommodation 106; language comprehension 127; physical impairments 103–104; into teaching sessions 39
catastrophising 16
central vision loss: effects on studying 63–64; symptoms 64
Charcot-Marie-Tooth disease (CMT) 94
children's academic inclusion 123
Christianity faith 124
chronic fatigue syndrome (CFS) 108
civil rights 8, 131; and disability 2–4
communication 24, 25, 29–34, 67, 114
conductive hearing loss 82–83; symptoms 83
Convention on the Rights of Persons with Disabilities (CRPD) 2
culturally sensitive language 127–128

D/deaf hearing impairments: additional vital information 90; case study 80–81; conductive hearing loss 82–83; group working 92–93; lip reading 87–89; mild hearing loss 84; mixed hearing loss 83–84; moderate hearing loss 84; neural hearing loss 84; non-medical help 89; personal emergency evacuation plan 91–92; sensorineural hearing loss 81–82; severe hearing loss 84–85
decision-making process 114
depression: definitions 39–40; dysthymia **41**; impact 39; mild depression **40**; moderate depression **40**; monolithic problem of 122; postnatal depression **41**; prenatal/antenatal depression **41**; seasonal affective disorder **40**; severe depression **40**; situational depression **41**; symptoms 39–40; types 39–41
depressive episodes **50**
deteriorating condition 115
dexamfetamine 20, **21**
Diagnostic and Statistical Manual of Mental Disorders (DSM-5) 17
difficulties writing, typing or notetaking. 17
disability 120–128; awareness 126–127; and civil rights 2–4; concept of 122–125; definition 1–2; Disability Discrimination Act (1995) 8; Equality Act 2010 8; Equal Pay Act 1970 8; history 7–8; intersectional discrimination 123; Judeo-Christian traditions 7; 1845 Lunacy Act 8; marginalise students 123; the medical and social models 4–6; medical model of 125; The 1601 Poor Law Act 8; Race Relations Act 1976 8; reasonable adjustments 9–10; Sex Discrimination Act 1975 8; social model of 130; UK legislation and statutory requirements 8–9
Disability Discrimination Act (1995) 8
disability support 110, 122, 129
disablism 6
diversity 96, 97, 125, 126, 129
The Diversity Style Guide (2021) 97
Durocher, J.S. 25
dyslexia: accessing resources 33; anxiety 16; assessments (accessible/alternative) 34; catastrophising 16; chief characteristics 24; course delivery 32; course design 31; definition 13–14; low motivation 16; low self-esteem 16; phonological processing 15; primary symptoms 14–15; secondary symptoms 15–16; self-management/personal organisation 15; working memory/information processing 15; written work 14–15
dyspraxia: accessing resources 33; assessments (accessible/alternative) 34; characteristics 17; chief characteristics 24; course delivery 32; course design 31; definition 16–17; fine motor coordination 17; gross motor coordination 17
dysthymia **41**

emergency intervention plan 112
emotional wellbeing 115
epileptics regulate 114
Equality Act 2010 8, 9, 125, 126
Equal Pay Act 1970 8
ethnic minority backgrounds 127

fatigue 6, 40, 66, 86, 94–96, 113, 115
field trip: care workers 106; date and time 106; educational activities 107; location 107; physiotherapy or medicine administration 107; travelling 106
fine motor coordination: difficulties writing, typing or notetaking 17; manual dexterity 17; poor handling/manipulative skills 17
fire emergency procedures 91
First World War 7
Fitzharris, L. 7
fluctuating conditions 111–112

gaps, education 115
gender preference 127
generalised anxiety disorder (GAD) **42**
genocide, Rwandan victims 122
glaucoma 64–66
Goodley, D. 6
Grandin, T. 6
Greene, P. 111
group working 79, 92–93
guanfacine 20, **22**
guide dogs 67, 68, 70, 71

Hammoud, M.M. 123
handouts/written material 90
Hawkes, J. 38
health anxiety (hypochondria) **45**
healthcare management 124
healthcare system 123
health, concept of 122–125
high blood pressure 108
higher education (HE) environments 122, 123; The Equality Act 2010 9; exams **54**; group work **53**; lectures/seminars **52**; personal organisation **55**; presentations **54**; reasonable adjustments 9–10; The Royal National Institute for the Blind material 68–69; staff-student relationship 56; student's attention 58; teaching and learning establishments 58; warm and welcoming environment 56
Hinduism faith 124

Historian Phillipa Vincent-Connolly's research 6

illness 120–128
impact on learning: executive dysfunction 18; information processing difficulties 17–18; instructions and multi-tasking 18
Institute for Medicine's Unequal Treatment: Confronting Racial and Ethnic Disparities in Health Care 123
institutional policy 110, 126
international human rights 2
International Labour Organization 2
international market 126
intersectional discrimination 123
irregular attendance 114
Islam faith 124

Jainism faith 124
Judaism faith 124

Karl case 61
Ketogenic diet 113
Kussmaul, A. 13

language comprehension 127
Lannister, T. 1
LGBTQ community 131
lifestyle factors 113–114
lip reading: adequately lit 88; body language 88; at a distance 89; multiple speakers 88; pitch and tone 88; signal 88; signpost topics 88; speaker's mouth 88; speech-to-text software 88–89; structure teaching sessions 88
lisdexamfetamine 20, **21**
Lister, K. Dr. 7, 20
literacy and language-related skills: phonological processing 15; self-management/personal organisation 15; working memory/information processing 15; written work 14–15
long-term medical condition: academic impact of 112–114; age 110; evidence, date of 110–111; fluctuating conditions 111–112; holistic approach 111; medical evidence 110; multiple diagnoses 111; student, difficulties 114–116; support plan 116–118
long-term self-management 112
low motivation 16
low self-esteem 16

Index

1845 Lunacy Act 8

macular degeneration 84
manic episodes **48–49**
manual dexterity 17
marginalise students 123
Martin, R.R. 1
medical evidence 110, 111, 112, 113
medication side effects 115
Melaku, T.M. 129
mental health: anticipatory adjustments 51–60; anxiety 41–46; bipolar disorder 48–50; case study 38–39; depression 39–41; environment and adjustments 50–51; issues 113; obsessive-compulsive disorder 46–47
methylphenidate 20, **21**
mild and moderate hearing loss 84
mild depression **40**
mixed hearing loss 83–84
moderate depression **40**
moderate hearing loss 84
Müller-Oerlinghausen, B. 48
multiple diagnoses 111
multiple sclerosis 115
muscular dystrophy 115

National Institute for Health and Care Excellence (NICE) 39
neural hearing loss 84
non-medical help: visually impaired/blind students 76
non-medical help (NMH): D/deaf hearing impairments 89
The Noonday Demon (Solomon) 122

obsession states 47
obsessive-compulsive disorder (OCD): chief characteristics 46; symptoms 47
Oliver, M. 5

panic attacks/disorder **43**
pastoral care and support: additional adjustments 58–59; conversation focuses 58; meeting 57–58; previously received support 59–60; receiving specialist support 59; role 58
peripheral (side) vision loss: effects on studying 65–66; symptoms 65
personal emergency evacuation plan (PEEP) 73; D/deaf hearing impairments 91–92; physical impairments 104–105; visually impaired/blind students 73

physical debilitation 113
physical discomfort 115
physical impairments: accommodation 102–103; care workers 103–104; case study 94–97; field trip 106–107; personal emergency evacuation plans 104–105; timetabling and accessible rooms 105–106; wheelchairs 97–102
physical mobility 112
poor handling/manipulative skills 17
The 1601 Poor Law Act 8
poor time management 15
postnatal depression (PND) **41**
post-traumatic stress disorder (PTSD) 38, **44**
prenatal/antenatal depression **41**
prenatal depression **41**
pre-registration assessment: accommodation visits 30; during induction/fresher's week 30; marketing and recruitment 29; pre-enrolment support plans 29–30; pre-entry events 29; quality assurance 29; routes of entry to HE 29
psychological trauma 121
public-facing webpage 66

Race Relations Act 1976 8
Rachael case 23
reading 77–78
recruitment and promotional materials 66–67
Richdale, A.L. 25
risk factors 113–114
room adjustments: equipment and non-medical help 75; equipment and support 75; functioning vision 75; power sockets 75; remove visual clutter 75; swivel chair 75; think lighting 75; visually impaired/blind students 75
Rose, J. 14
route planning and travelling 74
The Royal National Institute for the Blind (RNIB) 68–69
Rwandan Armed Forces 121
Rwandan Patriotic Front (RPF) 121

Saddiq case 80–82
Scope's 2018 Disability Perception Gap Policy Report 2
seasonal affective disorder (SAD) **40**
self-awareness 131
self-doubt 16, **50**

self-esteem 14, 16
self-management plan 112
self-recrimination 16
sensitive support plan 125; cultural beliefs 125; disability, understanding of 126; notions of disability 126
sensorineural hearing loss 81–82
severe depression 39, **40**, 51
severe hearing loss 84–85
Shakespeare, T. 1, 5
Shaywitz, B.A. 13
Shaywitz, S.E. 13
sighted guide: en route 69; first steps 68–69; initial approach 68; know your destination 69; non-medical help 76; uneven surfaces 69
sign language interpreter 89
situational depression **41**
Sjunneson, E. 6
Smith, J. 98
social anxiety disorder **43**
social collectivism 123
social model 129–131
society's purity laws 7
Solomon, Andrew 121
spoken taught sessions 88–89
Stacey, P. 6
staff/student childcare/allowances 123
stamina problems 115
stress and anxiety 16
student difficulties: anxiety 116; deteriorating condition 115; gaps, education 115; irregular attendance 114; stamina problems 115; unable to study 114–115
students: with allergies 112; difficulties 114–116; long-term self-management 112; medical evidence 114; missed teaching sessions 113; support plan 111; *see also individual entries*
support plan 111, 116–118; academic quality 117; accommodation 118; culturally sensitive language 127–128; disclosure and confidentiality 118; eating requirements 117; health declines 118; help with everyday living 118; inclusion plan 118; living arrangements 117; social life 117; student's expectations 116–117; student, university policy 118

taboo 120–128
Taoism 124
teaching: adjustments 77, 86; and learning 9, 31; living and social spaces 100; online teaching sessions 85; spaces **28,** 85; structure teaching sessions 88
timetabling and accessible rooms: accessible teaching space 105–106
Tim, T. 1

UK legislation 8–9
UK/western university model 123
unintentional violation 123
university disability service 125
university responsibilities: accommodation and interaction 71; spending pens/area 70; water bowls 71
unwritten effects 113

visually impaired/blind students 62; accessible recruitment practices 67–68; accessible rooms 73–75; accessible routes 73–75; accommodation adjustments 71–72; adjustment suggestions 78; blurred vision 63; case study 61; central vision loss 63–64; group work 79; guide dogs 70; non-medical help 76; notetakers support students 76; orientation and movement 68–69; peripheral (side) vision loss 64–66; personal emergency evacuation plan 73; reading 77–78; recruitment and promotional materials 66–67; room adjustments 75; teaching adjustments 77; university responsibilities 70–71; written work 79

western cultural evolution 123
wheelchair users: additional requirements 103; arrive on campus 100; campus/individual buildings 99; campus routes are accessible 100; core reading material 101; courses 100–101; Equality Act 2010 98; individual symptoms 99; nature of 99; personal assistants 102; pre-enrolment orientation visits 101; previous

experience 101; regular physiotherapy 102; student use 100
whispers/softly spoken speech 84
word blindness 13
World Health Organization (WHO) 39, 62

written work 79

Xuesong case 120

Youngstrom, E. A. 51